W9-BZW-828

**Kent Middle School
Media Center**

DEMCO

THE LINES ARE DRAWN

THE LINES ARE DRAWN

Political Cartoons
of the Civil War

Kristen M. Smith
EDITOR

Jennifer L. Gross
RESEARCH ASSISTANT

d

HILL STREET PRESS
ATHENS, GEORGIA

A HILL STREET PRESS BOOK

First printing

2 4 6 8 10 9 7 5 3 1

ISBN # 1-892514-06-0

Library of Congress Catalog Card Number: 98-75332

Hill Street Press is committed to preserving the written word.
Every effort is made to print books on acid-free paper with a significant amount of post-consumer recycled content.

Interior and cover design by Anne Richmond Boston.

Printed in the United States of America.

Published in the United States of America by
Hill Street Press LLC
191 East Broad Street, Suite 209
Athens, Georgia 30601-2848 USA
706-613-7200
info@hillstreetpress.com
www.hillstreetpress.com

CONTENTS

FOREWORD

Each year many of the major magazines in this country publish their "year-in-review" issues. One of the features of these issues, usually placed amid material that is important but less than titillating, are collections of the year's best editorial cartoons. What we have in *The Lines Are Drawn* is an equivalent enterprise for the entire American Civil War.

Editorial cartoons were relatively new to newspapers during the mid-nineteenth century. For over a century newspapers had relied upon techniques not unlike "clip art" to illustrate their editions. Then, during the 1850s developments in the technology of print made possible the display of drawings in media designed for the masses. Illustrations drawn by hand, often in the field, were made into woodcuts and then illustrations in print. The American Civil War was not only the first war to be photographed; it was the first war in which sketch artists could offer the readers of periodicals "action images" of soldiers on the march, in camp, and even in combat. These sketches were actually superior to the photographs of the time, because slow-shutter photography then required subjects to remain still for long periods and the photographer needed close proximity to darkrooms to develop still-wet collodial plates. As a result, photographers such as Matthew B. Brady, Alexander Gardner, and Timothy H. O'Sullivan could display dead soldiers aplenty, but live soldiers only in posed portraits, never in action. So pictures drawn and transformed into woodcuts were vital to mass media until the development of halftone illustration and news photography in the 1880s.

Today, sketches appear in print journalism only under special circumstances, such as depicting trials in which the judge prohibits the use of cameras in the courtroom. But editorial cartoons continue to be popular in the image-hungry culture of the present day in which colorful graphics and photographs otherwise dominate newspapers, magazines, and the Internet. So, in a sense, the cartoons shown here are "modern." The satire of *Southern Punch* and caricaturist Adalbert Johann Volck, as well as the cartoons of *Harper's Weekly* and Thomas Nast compare with the work of important editorial illustrators today such as Pulitzer Prize-winners Mike Luckovich of the *Atlanta Journal-Constitution* or Jeff MacNelly of the *Chicago Tribune*.

Cartoonists in the nineteenth century were seldom subtle and the work reproduced here includes some pretty crude caricature and polemics. Racism was rampant in the period, and Southern slaveholders had no monopoly. *The London Punch* and numerous Northern cartoonists looked upon African Americans as inferior and spared no ink in saying so. In addition, anti-Semitism was common and often revealed, as was ethnic prejudice against Irish and other peoples. Accordingly, a sample of cartoons in this volume display a black "Sambo" taking his ease, a Jewish "Shylock" extorting his neighbors, or a Irish "Paddy" in drunken search of a brawl.

The cartoons collected here may or may not reflect the majority opinion of the day. Of course, artists usually react to the world around them and depict their interpretation of that world. The North had more numerous and more broadly circulated illustrated newspapers than did the South from the beginning, and because the United States ultimately won the war, illustrations produced in the North have had a better survival rate. Thus, for various reasons, more pro-Northern cartoons than pro-Southern cartoons are included.

These disclaimers seem minor when contrasted with the value of the entire corpus. This is good stuff, art for the masses, that continues to amuse and enlighten viewers and readers to this day.

Enjoy.

Emory M. Thomas
Athens, Georgia

ACKNOWLEDGMENTS

I am especially grateful to the following people: Tom Payton, for suggesting the idea of this book and for his guidance and patience; Anne Richmond Boston, for the beautiful design of the book; Patrick Allen, for the apt title; and Jean-Pierre Caillault, for his good humor and support.

The following librarians, archivists, and staff members at the University of Georgia Libraries deserve my special thanks: Shelia McAlister, Nelson Morgan, Nan McMurry, Marilyn Healy, Danny Bridges, and Katie Brower. Thank you, Tim Murray, for pointing me in the right direction for so many years. I owe a tremendous debt of gratitude to Mary Ellen Brooks, director of the Hargrett Rare Book and Manuscript Library, who acts as a fine steward of documents important to Southern and national culture. Her assistance was invaluable in making this book possible.

I appreciate the assistance provided by the following individuals and institutions: Terri Hudgins at the Museum of the Confederacy; Rob Schoeberlein at the Maryland Historical Society Library; Wayne Furman and Mark Andres at the New York Public Library; and Anne Easterling at the Museum of the City of New York.

Finally, thank you to Emory Thomas for his foreword, which sets the perfect stage for the collection. And thanks to Jennifer Gross for her scholarly expertise.

Kristen M. Smith

INTRODUCTION

Most of the cartoons in this collection were selected from illustrated weekly papers published during the Civil War and from lithographs which could be purchased individually from printers. Across the Atlantic, *Punch* appeared in London in 1841 and served as a model for many American papers. The mid-1850s marked the beginning of illustrated weeklies in New York such as *Frank Leslie's Illustrated Newspaper, Harper's Weekly*, and the *New York Illustrated News*. These three publications had a combined circulation of over one-quarter million, and each issue was probably read by several people per household or business. The Southern imitations of these papers—*Southern Punch* and the *Southern Illustrated News*—began in the early 1860s when the war kept Northern papers out of the South. These illustrated papers relied on wood engravings to reproduce cartoons, which could appear in record time—a few weeks after the events to which they referred.

The Lines Are Drawn begins with lithographs from Currier & Ives on the topic of the 1860 presidential election. Currier & Ives was founded in New York City by Nathaniel Currier, who later took James Ives as his partner. To produce a lithograph in the mid-1800s, the artist drew on a limestone slab with a wax crayon. When ink was applied to the stone, the ink adhered to the waxy areas, was repelled by the other areas, and made a faithful print on paper. Currier & Ives printed some eighty black-and-white political cartoons in addition to their famous hand-colored prints. These could be purchased individually—in the printer's showroom or at political party headquarters—and some election-year lithographs had print runs as large as 100,000 (Hess and Kaplan, 1968). Several artists often contributed to a single print. These artists included Louis Maurer, Ben Day, John Cameron, Thomas Worth, and Currier himself who often did not sign his name to his work. The lithographs in this collection (and some are from printers other than Currier & Ives) are qualitatively different from the cartoons that ran in the weekly newspapers. The litho images, which were made on a stone slab, often featured stone-like characters. The lithographs have a certain lifelessness, which might come from the fact that the characters' faces were drawn realistically from posed photographs. Also contributing to the stiltedness of these drawings are the jam-packed word balloons that float at the top of the cartoons.

The Lines Are Drawn is arranged in chronological order and the source of the cartoon and the name of the artist are provided when known. All the cartoons from the British weekly *Punch* were drawn by Sir John Tenniel (famous for his *Alice in Wonderland* illustrations), whose style is unmistakable and who usually signed his name with a symbol that combined his initials. Frank Bellew, whose cartoon of an exceptionally tall Abe Lincoln might be the most widely remembered cartoon of its time, worked for *Frank Leslie's Illustrated Newspaper* and signed his cartoons with a triangle. Also working at *Frank Leslie's Illustrated Newspaper* was Thomas Nast, who began his job there at the age of fifteen and was barely twenty when the Civil War began. From 1858 to 1862, in addition to working for *Frank Leslie's*, he freelanced for *Harper's Weekly* and the *New York Illustrated News*. In 1862 he joined the staff of *Harper's Weekly*, where he went on to do his most famous work. Nast signed his illustrations and many of his cartoons *Th. Nast*, but sometimes he signed the cartoons with only an *N*. This *N* was sometimes fanciful, sometimes plain. I can only guess at reasons for the inconsistent signings. Maybe he was experimenting, maybe he feared overexposure since he worked for several papers, or maybe he meant to distinguish his simpler cartoons from his complex illustrations. William Murrell, in his book *A History of American Graphic Humor*, discovered another cartoonist, William Newman, who also signed his name with an *N,* and who worked at *Frank Leslie's Illustrated Newspaper* during Nast's tenure there. Cartoons after 1862 from *Frank Leslie's* signed only with an *N* can be fairly assumed to be Newman's, but prior to 1862 there is some uncertainty as to what work is Newman's and what is Nast's.

The most notable Southern cartoonist was Baltimore dentist Adalbert Johann Volck. Dentist by day, artist by night, Volck produced the most scathing portrayals of Lincoln seen during the war. Volck signed his etchings *V. Blada*—the first initial of his last name and a partial palindrome of his first name—and he published his *Confederate War Etchings* in 1863 under a fake London imprint.

It is unfortunate that many of the cartoons in this collection are unsigned or signed only with initials. Little is known about the artists of these cartoons. Other cartoonists working at this time included Henry Stephens (*Harper's Weekly*), Frank Beard (*Harper's* and *Leslie's*), Matt Morgan (*Leslie's*), Arthur Lumley (*New York Illustrated News*), and David Strother (*Southern Punch*).

Readers will notice a marked difference in style between the cartoons from the illustrated weekly newspapers in the North and those in the South. Northern cartoons are mostly well executed and have a sensibility similar to political cartoons today. The Southern cartoons, with a few notable exceptions, such as the etchings of Adalbert Volck, are crudely drawn, and the ideas are often not as well crafted as their Northern counterparts. There are several reasons for this. First, the North had a thriving publishing industry, whereas the South did not. When the war began, the South was cut off from the Northern weeklies and suffered paper and ink shortages. Richmond, Virginia was the publishing center of the South, but engravers and lithographers there were busy producing official images, currency, stamps, and documents related to establishing the Confederate States of America (C.S.A.) as a new nation. Still, out of Richmond came the only two sources of regularly published political cartoons from the Southern perspective: *Southern Punch* and the *Southern Illustrated News*. The *Southern Illustrated News* published its first issue in September 1862 and *Southern Punch* began in August 1863; they each lasted about two years. Both papers were inferior imitations of the Northern weeklies, and they were not above swiping an occasional cartoon from their Northern rivals and changing it to suit their needs. An example is the cartoon on page 20 in which Lincoln is shown as a cabinetmaker. In this cartoon the caption was changed, the signature removed, and facial hair added to Lincoln reflecting his then-new and now-famous beard. It is interesting to note that as late as 1863,

Southern cartoonists occasionally forgot to draw Lincoln's beard (see page 84 and page 86). The reason for this oversight might be that along with other shortages, Southern cartoonists did not have access to many photographs of the U.S. president. Whatever the reasons for the differences in presentation and cartooning acumen between the North and the South, cartoonists in the North were masters of their craft, while their Southern counterparts lagged behind.

Many symbols recur in the cartoons, and I will mention a few in case some readers are unfamiliar with them. Columbia is the female personification of the United States and was named after Christopher Columbus. She symbolized the American people until the appearance of Brother Jonathan, who became Uncle Sam. The reader can observe the evolution of Uncle Sam, and notice the way artists, especially John Tenniel, incorporated the features of Lincoln into this national symbol. John Bull, a stout gentleman often drawn with a top hat and cane, is the English counterpart of Uncle Sam and appears in many cartoons. Much is made in the early cartoons of Lincoln's rail-splitting days. He is often shown with split rails or with tools such as a maul. These symbolize Lincoln's honest, hardworking background in Illinois before he entered politics. Conversely, the scotch plaid cap and overcoat often associated with Lincoln (and explained in the book) are signifiers of cowardice.

Several cartoons at the end of the book paint a hopeful picture of a reunified nation moving ahead strong and free. This optimism is both inspiring and naive as we consider the resistance to Reconstruction in the South and the very little change seen in the lives of African Americans after the war, except for the psychological and semantic differences between being enslaved and being putatively free.

This brings me to the fact that cartoonists use stereotypes as a type of shorthand, and that there are racist portrayals of nationalities and especially of African Americans in this collection. I know they will cause discomfort for many readers. I have included cartoons with these offensive images because they reflect a segment of popular view of their time and, in the case of African Americans, because slavery was such a pivotal issue in the war and in the history of the United States.

To my knowledge, no women contributed cartoons to this collection.

As you read, remember that cartoons are open to interpretation. I hope that you as a reader discover humor, symbolism, and meanings for yourself in *The Lines Are Drawn.*

Kristen M. Smith
Athens, Georgia

Hess, Stephen and Milton Kaplan. *The Ungentlemanly Art: A History of American Political Cartoons.* New York: The Macmillan Company, 1968.

Holzer, Harold. "Confederate Caricature of Abraham Lincoln." *Illinois Historical Journal* 80 (1987): 23-36.

Murrell, William. *A History of American Graphic Humor: 1865–1938.* New York: The Macmillan Company, 1938.

Somers Jr., Paul P. *Editorial Cartooning and Caricature: A Reference Guide.* Connecticut: Greenwood Press, 1998.

Thompson Jr., William Fletcher. "Pictorial Images of the Negro During the Civil War." *Wisconsin Magazine of History* 48 (1965): 282-294.

1860

THE GREAT MATCH AT BALTIMORE,
BETWEEN THE "ILLINOIS BANTAM", AND THE "OLD COCK" OF THE WHITE HOUSE.

THE GREAT MATCH AT BALTIMORE

⇥⇥ 1860 ⇤⇤

Feathers fly in this portrayal of the Democratic convention in Baltimore in 1860, where a divided party nomi- nated Stephen Douglas for president. Douglas is shown as a victorious, diminutive rooster atop incumbent James Buchanan. Entering the ring at right is a wary rooster with the head of Vice President John Breckinridge. A small-headed Irishman, probably representing immigrants of the Tammany Democratic machine in New York City, gives his commentary on the fight.

Currier & Ives
Artist: probably Louis Maurer

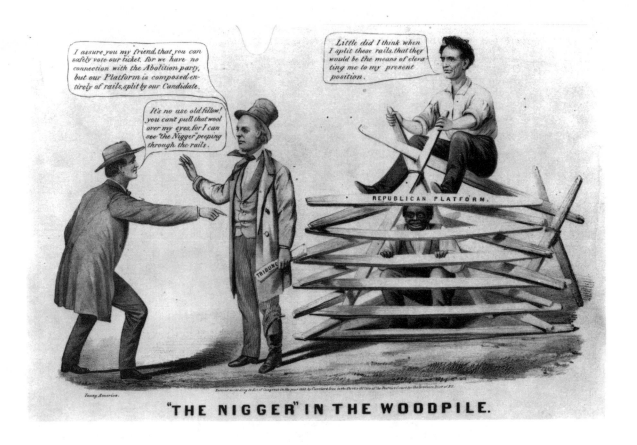

"THE NIGGER" IN THE WOODPILE

"THE NIGGER" IN THE WOODPILE

⟜≡ 1860 ≡⟝

Republican efforts to minimize the role of abolition in the party's platform are ridiculed in this cartoon.

Horace Greeley, editor of the *New York Tribune*, tells a young American that the Republicans are not affiliated with the Abolition party. The young American points to a black man peering out of a structure made of rails, one of which is, in fact, labeled "Republican Platform." Sitting on the rails is Abraham Lincoln, the 1860 Republican presidential candidate.

Currier & Ives
Artist: probably Louis Maurer

THE POLITICAL QUADRILLE

Music by Dred Scott

THE POLITICAL QUADRILLE

⊰⊶ 1860 ⊷⊱

The presidential candidates dance around the issue of slavery with their supposed allies: upper left, John Breckinridge and incumbent James Buchanan; upper right, Lincoln dances with an African American woman; lower left, Stephen Douglas cavorts with a tattered Irishman; and lower right, Constitutional Union party candidate John Bell dances with a Native American brave. Dred Scott—a former slave whose case before the Supreme Court resulted in the 1857 decision that the Missouri Compromise was unconstitutional and that slaves were not citizens of any state or the United States—plays the fiddle.

Printer unknown
Artist unknown

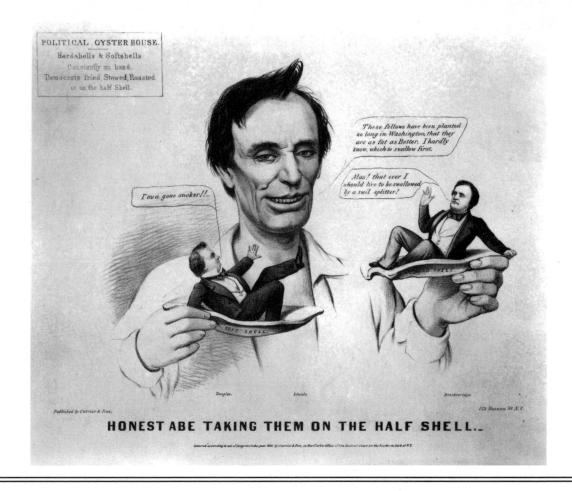

HONEST ABE TAKING THEM ON THE HALF SHELL

⊷⊶ 1860 ⊷⊶

Democrats were referred to as either soft-shell (moderate on slavery) or hard-shell (pro-slavery). In this cartoon, Lincoln tries to decide which Democrat on a half shell to eat first: Northern nominee Stephen Douglas on the left or Southern nominee John Breckinridge on the right.

Currier & Ives
Artist: probably Louis Maurer

THE RAIL CANDIDATE

⋙ 1860 ⋘

Lincoln straddles a rail labeled "Republican Platform" in an allusion to the uncomfortable and controversial antislavery plank of the 1860 Republican campaign. One end of the rail is supported by a slave, while the other is held by Horace Greeley.

Currier & Ives
Artist: probably Louis Maurer

STORMING THE CASTLE

STORMING THE CASTLE

⊷ 1860 ⊷

Lincoln dressed as a Wide-Awake (a marching club of young Republican men, who carried lanterns and wore capes and visors) rounds the corner of the White House to find other candidates trying to get inside. Incumbent James Buchanan tries to help his vice president, John Breckinridge, through a window. Democrat Stephen Douglas attempts to open the door with keys labeled "Non Intervention," "Regular Nomination," and "Nebraska Bill." John Bell, the Constitutional Union party candidate, keeps watch as Lincoln approaches.

Currier & Ives
Artist: Louis Maurer

LINCOLN AND DOUGLAS IN A PRESIDENTIAL FOOTRACE

~=◉ 1860 ◉=~

Lincoln and Douglas race for the presidency and towards the U.S. Capitol. Lincoln's tallness and Douglas's shortness have been exaggerated giving Lincoln an advantage. Lincoln carries a rail splitter's maul, and Douglas carries a cane on which hangs a jug labeled "M.C." for the Missouri Compromise, which prohibited slavery in Kansas and Nebraska and was repealed in 1854 by the Kansas-Nebraska Act presented by Douglas. A black man calls to Douglas from the fence to remind him of the issue of slavery in the campaign.

J. Sage & Sons
Artist unknown

CONGRESSIONAL SURGERY, LEGISLATIVE QUACKERY

⚬⚬⚬ 1860 ⚬⚬⚬

This anti-North cartoon derides proposed constitutional amendments to curtail slavery in the states. "Dr. North" (Pennsylvania Congressman Thaddeus Stevens) sits in a chair facing his patient—a man representing the South with his arm in a sling. A black person lies on the floor next to the chair. On the desk between the doctor and patient is a wooden leg labeled, "Constitutional Amendment."

Printer unknown
Signed: A. Del

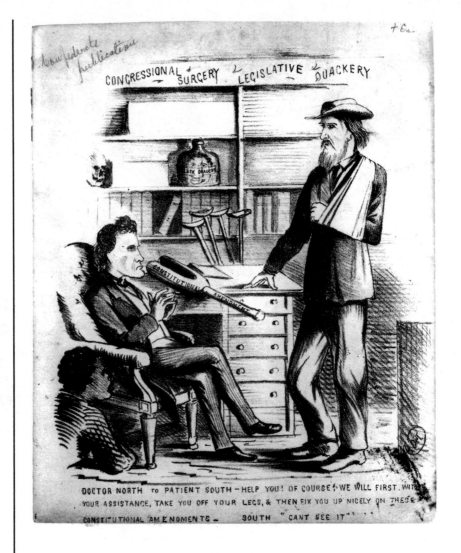

1861

SOUTH CAROLINA'S "ULTIMATUM".

SOUTH CAROLINA'S "ULTIMATUM"

⇾≡ 1861 ≡⇽

Francis Pickens, governor of the newly seceded state of South Carolina, stands in front of a cannon labeled "Peace Maker" and threatens to light it unless lame-duck President Buchanan surrenders Fort Sumter. The cannon faces Pickens, suggesting that a war between the South and the United States would be suicide.

Currier & Ives
Artist unknown

Divorce à Vinculo

—≡≈ 1861 ≈≡—

South Carolina and the Union are represented as a couple who are breaking the ties of marriage over South Carolina's right to handle slaves as she likes.

Punch
(January 19)
Artist: Sir John Tenniel

DIVORCE À VINCULO.

Mrs. Carolina Asserts her Right to "Larrup" her Nigger.

"HARK FROM THE *TOOMBS* A DOLEFUL CRY."

TOOMBS OF THE SECESSIONISTS

◆═ 1861 ═◆

C.S.A. Secretary of State Robert Toombs was an early advocate of Secession when he was a U.S. senator. This cartoon warns of a grisly fate for those who would abandon the Union. Toombs was seriously wounded at the Battle of Antietam in 1862, where he served as Brigadier General in the Georgia Brigade, but he recovered and later served in the Georgia militia during Sherman's "march to the sea."

New York Illustrated News
(January 19)
Artist unknown

THE "SECESSION MOVEMENT".

THE "SECESSION MOVEMENT"

⇥ 1861 ⇤

Four men representing Southern states ride donkeys and follow South Carolina in pursuit of a butterfly labeled "Secession Humbug." This group riding toward Secession is about to gallop over a cliff. A fifth man, who represents Georgia, veers away from the group saying, "We have some doubts about *the end* of that road and think it expedient to deviate a little."

Currier & Ives
Artist unknown

THE FOLLY OF SECESSION.

THE FOLLY OF SECESSION

–⇒ 1861 ⇐–

In this cartoon, a cow represents the Union. Pulling on its tail is South Carolina Governor Francis Pickens, a leading proponent of Secession. Pulling on its horns is outgoing President James Buchanan. A man representing Georgia milks the cow into a bucket labeled "City of Savannah," which may allude to that state's seizure of federal Fort Pulaski at Savannah on January 3.

Currier & Ives
Artist unknown

LITTLE BO-PEEP AND HER FOOLISH SHEEP.

"*Little Bo-peep, she lost her sheep,* | *Let 'em alone, and they'll all come home,*
And didn't know where to find 'em; | *With their tails hanging down behind 'em.*"

LITTLE BO-PEEP AND HER FOOLISH SHEEP

1861

Columbia dressed as Little Bo-Peep looks on as seven of her sheep run into a forest of Palmetto trees. The Palmetto is the symbol of South Carolina, and one wayward sheep is labeled "S.C." Wolves wearing crowns and representing European powers threaten the sheep. Columbia commands a dog named Old Buck, i.e. James Buchanan, to protect the sheep, but he flees in the opposite direction. A dog named Old Hickory lies dead on the ground and represents President Andrew Jackson, a supporter of a strong Union.

Thomas W. Strong, printer
Artist unknown

Passage through Baltimore

⇥ 1861 ⇤

While Lincoln was en route to his first inauguration, he was informed of a "Baltimore Plot" to assassinate him. He was persuaded to rearrange his plans and take a night train to Baltimore where he then changed railroads and continued to Washington. Lincoln was said to have disguised himself in a large overcoat and cap. The press embellished this story and reported that Lincoln had worn a Scotch plaid cap and a long military cloak. After this incident, cartoonists used these props when they wanted to mock Lincoln. In this cartoon, Lincoln and a cat frighten each other.

Confederate War Etchings
Artist: V. Blada (Adalbert Johann Volck)

UNION GLUE

⇥═ 1861 ═⇤

During the lame duck presidency of Buchanan, seven states withdrew from the Union. In December, South Carolina seceded. Ordinances of Secession were then passed in January by Mississippi, Florida, Alabama, Georgia, and Louisiana and by Texas in February. This cartoon, from *Southern Punch*, ran first in *Frank Leslie's Illustrated Newspaper* with the original, less partisan caption, "A Job for the New Cabinet Maker." The original cartoon was signed H. D. and showed a beardless Lincoln.

Southern Punch
Also in **Frank Leslie's Illustrated Newspaper**
(February 2)
Signed: H. D. (Howard Del)

Lincoln vainly, endeavoring to cement the old Union.

OLD ABE—" *Oh, it's all well enough to say, that I must support the dignity of my high office by Force—but it's darned uncomfortable sitting—I can tell yer.*"

OLD ABE'S UNCOMFORTABLE SEAT

⇢ 1861 ⇠

Lincoln is in an uncomfortable position sitting on bayonets. He laments that it's unpleasant to use force to support the dignity of the presidency and the Union.

Frank Leslie's Illustrated Newspaper
(March 2)
Artist unknown

This is the way the North receives it.

THE PRESIDENT'S INAUGURAL,
And

This is the way the South receives it

The President's Inaugural

⇒≡ 1861 ≡⇐

During Lincoln's inaugural address on March 4, he declared, "We are not enemies, but friends." This cartoon represents extreme Northern and Southern views of Lincoln's inauguration. At left, Lincoln is Justice bringing peace to the North and South. At right, Lincoln is a warring gladiator threatening the smaller South.

New York Illustrated News
(March 23)
Artist: Thomas Nast

STRONG'S DIME CARICATURES—No. 4

⟐ 1861 ⟐

This cartoon represents the hopeful idea that Lincoln might end the Secession movement in the Southern states. Lincoln, a schoolmaster dressed like Uncle Sam, scolds boys playing in a mudhole labeled "secession." He wants them to behave, and reminds them that they set a bad example for the other boys (border states) sitting and playing in the background. Lincoln holds a little girl representing South Carolina, who bites him in an effort to get free. On the ground is a flag of South Carolina, a soldier's hat, and a toy gun.

*Thomas W. Strong, Printer
(March)
Artist: probably John H. Goater*

"Cæsar Imperator!" or The American Gladiators

1861

Though the North claimed the preservation of the Union and the South claimed the enforcement of states rights as their respective causes, observers abroad and various segments of the populace saw the war as a contest over the slaves.

Punch
(May 18)
Artist: Sir John Tenniel

"CÆSAR IMPERATOR!"
OR,
THE AMERICAN GLADIATORS.

COLUMBIA AWAKE AT LAST.

COLUMBIA AWAKE AT LAST

⊷⊷ 1861 ⊷⊷

Columbia throttles the Confederacy, who holds a piece of the Constitution he has torn away. His legs are labeled "treason" and "secession." Two startled Confederate soldiers look on from the background. Fort Sumpter (sic) can be seen at left. The Confederates fired on Fort Sumter on April 12, and the Civil War began. Both the Union and the Confederacy used George Washington's ideas as a justification for their causes. This cartoonist puts Washington in the Union's camp.

Harper's Weekly
(June 8)
Artist unknown

THE SOUTHERN
CONFEDERACY—AN
ALLEGORICAL
ILLUSTRATION

⤞══ 1861 ══⤝

In this cartoon, the Southern Confederacy—and by extension, the economy of the Confederacy, which was based on cotton production—is carried on the back of a slave. The Confederacy is represented as a bomb with a lighted fuse.

New York Illustrated News
(July 15)
Artist unknown

THE SOUTHERN CONFEDERACY—AN ALLEGORICAL ILLUSTRATION. By
our Serious Contributor.—See page 172.

Fancy Sketch of Right Reverend Major-General Bishop Polk heading his "Division."

C.S.A. General and Episcopal Bishop Leonidas Polk was a friend and classmate of Jefferson Davis's. He was appointed Major General in June of 1861. His appointment was primarily symbolic. In this cartoon he rides, in full cleric attire, over a scroll labeled "Church Canon."

Harper's Weekly
(July 27)
Artist: Thomas Nast

A MILD SHOCK FOR OUR VIRTUOUS FRIEND, MR. JOHN BULL.

A MILD SHOCK FOR OUR VIRTUOUS FRIEND, MR. JOHN BULL

⊸⊜ 1861 ⊜⊷

A black jack-in-the box surprises John Bull (Britain) with the threat of "No More Cotton." The South hoped that Lincoln's blockade of Southern ports would work in their favor since the British and French economies depended on Southern cotton. The South wanted England and France to recognize the Confederacy and come to its aid.

Harper's Weekly
(August 3)
Signed: J. H. H.

AN UNWELCOME RETURN.

THREE MONTHS' VOLUNTEER. "What! don't you know me—your own husband?"
DAUGHTER OF COLUMBIA. "Get away! No husband of mine would be here while the country needs his help."

AN UNWELCOME RETURN

⇢⇒ 1861 ⇐⇠

This cartoon is enlistment propaganda playing on ideas of what a partriotic man should be. A "Daughter of Columbia" rejects her husband who is returning from three months in the Union army, saying: "Get away! No husband of mine would be here while the country needs his help."

Harper's Weekly
(August 10)
Artist unknown

Pennsylvania Beef Contractor

⸺⊷ 1861 ⊷⸺

During the early years of the war, numerous charges of profiteering arose against Northern capitalists including textile manufacturers, gun suppliers, railroads, and food producers. Cartoonists often made references to the shoddy condition of soldiers' uniforms and shoes and the inadequacy of their diets, blaming such deficiencies on disloyal profiteers.

Harper's Weekly
(August 17)
Artist: Thomas Nast

PENNSYLVANIA BEEF CONTRACTOR. "Want Beefsteak? Good Gracious, what is the World coming to? Why, my Good Fellow, if you get Beefsteak, how on earth are Contractors to live? Tell me that."

OLD MOSES DAVIS TO PRINCE NAPOLEON.

" Now, my dear poy, come over to our side—don't go to the old man on de utter side of de vay. Ve vill let you have de cotton at your own price—sheap. Come, my poy !"

OLD MOSES DAVIS TO PRINCE NAPOLEON

⊷≡ 1861 ≡⊶

In 1861, Confederate officials and Southerners as a whole were confident that they could depend on support from England and France in their efforts to establish a country independent of the United States since both countries were dependent on Southern cotton for their textile mills. Here "Old Moses" Davis uses a French accent to try to woo Napoleon III, Emporer of France, promising him all the cotton he could ever want. At right, Lincoln broods outside the White House.

New York Illustrated News
(August 19)
Artist: Thomas Nast

THE OPPONENTS OF THE "UNNATURAL AND FRATRICIDAL WAR."

"Mr. Breckinridge offered a Petition, signed by 600 Citizens of Niagara County, New York, deprecating Civil War as leading to Disunion, and asking Congress to pass Amendments to the Constitution, or call immediately a National Convention."—*Proceedings of Congress.*

The Opponents of the "Unnatural and Fratricidal War"

⇢⇢ 1861 ⇠⇠

John Breckinridge, as a Southern Democrat, was one of the four presidential candidates in 1860. After Lincoln won the election, Breckinridge worked in the Senate to promote a compromise to the war. When his efforts were unsuccessful, he joined the Confederate Army as a brigadier general. In this cartoon, Lincoln, as a gambler, leads a motley crew opposed to war.

Harper's Weekly
(August 24)
Artist unknown

A HINT FOR GENERAL M'CLELLAN.

"After we had hanged a few contractors, I am bound to say that the quality of beef served out to the troops improved amazingly."—SIR C. NAPIER'S *Dispatches.*

A HINT FOR GENERAL MCCLELLAN

↔══ 1861 ══↔

Another reference to wartime profiteering, only this time it implicates General George McClellan along with Northern capitalists. Here, McClellan looks on as a capitalist is hanged by all the money that he made at the expense of Union soldiers.

Harper's Weekly
(*August 24*)
Signed: J. H. H

THE VOLUNTARY MANNER IN WHICH SOME OF THE SOUTHERN VOLUNTEERS ENLIST.

THE VOLUNTARY MANNER IN WHICH SOME OF THE SOUTHERN VOLUNTEERS ENLIST

⇌ 1861 ⇌

This cartoon mocks the South's efforts to raise an army. A poorly dressed man is being encouraged by the tips of three bayonets to enlist as a volunteer. Equally shabby is the interior of the recruitment office, where an officer sits at a desk made from a whiskey barrel. A drunken man is propped against a wall, and a small dog urinates on him.

Currier & Ives
Artist: Thomas Worth and Del

GREAT RISE IN BEEF

⤛⟜ 1861? ⟞⤜

An allusion to the high cost of meat in the Confederacy: "Oh Lord, I wish you were not quite so high."

Southern Punch
Date unknown
Artist unknown

Entered according to Act of Congress by Wiswell in the Clerks office of the Southern District of Ohio June 18th 1861.

SECESSION EXPLODED

⚬⚬ 1861 ⚬⚬

A sea monster representing the Secession movement is blasted by a cannon that is fired by Uncle Sam and labeled "Death to Traitors!" The monster explodes into smaller fantastical creatures representing states that had seceded or that were divided. Included is Tennessee senator John Bell, an 1860 presidential candidate. A two-faced creature (Baltimore) grabs onto Lincoln's coattails as a reminder that while Maryland never left the Union many residents sympathized with the South. Winfield Scott, Union commander, rests on an American flag on the shore.

Printer unknown
Artist unknown

THE RIP VAN WINKLE OF THE NAVY DEPARTMENT IN SLEEPY HOLLOW.
"These Privateers are really becoming annoying. I think I must buy a Tug-boat."

THE RIP VAN WINKLE OF THE NAVY DEPARTMENT IN SLEEPY HOLLOW

⇢⊚ 1861 ⊚⇠

Gideon Welles, Union Secretary of the Navy, was loyal to Lincoln and served with efficiency, but in this cartoon he is asleep on the job. Two boats approach the shore: John Bull and a load of cotton are in one boat, and Napoleon III and a crate of cigars are in another. At first the Confederacy was successful in evading the Union blockade. Eventually, Welles and the Union Navy woke up and put an end to Southern blockade running.

Harper's Weekly
(August 31)
Artist unknown

THE BRAVE STAY-AT-HOME "LIGHT GUARD"

⇥ 1861 ⇤

When the Union army lost at the first battle of Bull Run in 1861, it was all the more inglorious because the retreat was a full fledged flight. The womanly costume in this cartoon mocks not only those Northerners who would not enlist, but also those who had proved their cowardice in the face of battle.

Harper's Weekly
(September 7)
Artist unknown

Costume suggested for the Brave STAY-AT-HOME "LIGHT GUARD."

"RECOGNITION," or "NO."

J. BULL *to* NAPOLEON III. "Can you recognize that thing they call the C. S. A.?"
NAP. "Well, I think I could, if 'twere not for that Big Fellow who stands in front."

"RECOGNITION" OR "NO"

⤖ 1861 ⬸

John Bull and Napoleon III stand on ground labeled "Europe." Across the water, on a shore labeled "America,"

Lincoln holds a U.S. flag and eclipses a smaller figure in the distance behind him holding a flag that reads "C.S.A." If England and France recognized the Confederate States of America, they would have put themselves at risk for war with the United States.

Harper's Weekly
(September 14)
Artist: Thomas Nast

The Hercules of the Union

⊷⇒ 1861 ⇐⊷

This cartoon pays homage to Union General Winfield Scott, a hero of the War of 1812 and the war with Mexico. Here, he is portrayed as Hercules slaying the many-headed Hydra from Greek mythology (Secession). Each head of the Hydra represents a Southern leader and his crime. From the bottom: John B. Floyd, Secretary of War under Buchanan; Francis Pickens, governor of South Carolina; General David E. Twiggs; Army commander P. G. T. Beauregard; President Jefferson Davis; Vice President Alexander Stephens; and Confederate Secretary of State Robert Toombs.

Printer unknown

Artist unknown

GENERAL SCOTT.

THE HERCULES OF THE UNION,
SLAYING THE GREAT DRAGON OF SECESSION.

The SACHEM of TAMMANY Kicking Out a WOOD(en) Imitation of Democracy.

THE SACHEM OF TAMMANY

⇢ 1861 ⇠

The New York County Democratic Society of Tammany was an oath-bound political society formed in 1783 and organized in 1789 to uphold the tenets of democracy in the United States. Many of the society's rituals were patterned after Native American customs. Northern voters, like those who belonged to Tammany Hall, were unwilling to accept a democracy that left them beholden to the power of Southern planters. Accordingly, they supported the war.

Harper's Weekly
(September 21)
Signed: J. H. H.

John Bull Since the Southern Rebellion

⊷ 1861 ⊶

John Bull kicks a black man out of Exeter Hall in England. The black man carries a sign bearing the motto of the Anti-Slavery Society of London. On the ground is a placard bearing the name W. Wilberforce, a British statesman who secured passage in 1807 of a bill abolishing the slave trade. In the foreground is Harriet Beecher Stowe's novel, *Uncle Tom's Cabin*, which had a powerful abolitionist influence. This cartoon mocks England for considering recognizing the Confederacy—contradicting its anti-slavery stance—for the sake of cotton.

Harper's Weekly
(September 28)
Artist unknown

JOHN BULL SINCE THE SOUTHERN REBELLION.

A FAMILY QUARREL.

A FAMILY QUARREL

→═ 1861 ═←

The war is portrayed as a domestic dispute. The South shakes her fist at the North while each holds half of a torn U.S. map. Broken furniture is strewn around, and in the background a racist caricature of the happy, childish slave is shown tiptoeing away from the quarrel. This cartoon suggests that the issue of slavery was intimately involved in the war, despite what the opposing sides said.

Punch

(September 28)

Artist: Sir John Tenniel

GOT THE RIGHT WEAPON AT LAST

➤➤ 1861 ➤➤

While the Confederacy relied on loans for almost two-thirds of its war finances, the Federal government raised two-thirds of its military revenue in this manner through short-term loans at 7.3% interest and longer term bonds at 6% interest. In this cartoon, Union loan policies are on the verge of toppling the Confederate war effort portrayed as a house of cards.

Harper's Weekly
(October 19)
Artist: Thomas Nast

GOT THE RIGHT WEAPON AT LAST.

OLD SECESH CROSSING THE POTOMAC.

This River is hard to Cross. If I can keep my Head above Water, however, a little longer, some of my Foreign Friends will recognize me and lend a hand. Meantime, I can go neither Forward nor Backward.

A Southern character representing Secession is submerged up to his neck in the Potomac between Virginia and Washington. Dangerous sea creatures circle around him. He hopes that England, France, and Spain will recognize him and come to his aid if he holds out a little longer. The longer the Confederacy remained independent, the easier it would be for other countries to recognize the new nation. Also the South assumed that as time passed, the European need for cotton would increase.

Harper's Weekly
(October 19)
Artist: Thomas Nast

Jeff Davis Reaping the Harvest

⊶⊷ 1861 ⊶⊷

A monstrous Jeff Davis, scythe in hand, gathers a harvest of human skulls. In the background a buzzard sits on a tree from which a noose (for Davis) hangs. This cartoon suggests the fate of the South and of Southerners if the war continued.

Harper's Weekly
(October 26)
Artist: Frank Bellew

JEFF DAVIS REAPING THE HARVEST.

A "SMASH" FOR JEFF.

A "SMASH" FOR JEFF

⇒ 1861 ⇐

In 1861 and the early part of 1862, some of the Union's most important victories were won at sea rather than on land. The success of the federal naval blockade as well as the capture of several important Southern ports effectively crippled the South's efforts to receive supplies from the outside world. Though Southerners crowed about early successes in running the blockade, the Confederacy was sitting on a powder keg when it came to outwitting the larger and more experienced U.S. navy.

Harper's Weekly
(November 2)
Artist: Frank Bellew

INDIAN COTTON DEPÔT

COTTON STORES

OVER THE WAY.

Mr Bull. "OH! IF YOU TWO LIKE FIGHTING BETTER THAN BUSINESS, I SHALL DEAL AT **THE OTHER SHOP**."

OVER THE WAY

⇒ 1861 ⇐

Although England had for some time relied on Southern cotton for its textile mills, the Confederacy was incorrect to think that England would join the war against the Union simply for the sake of cotton. Ultimately, the Civil War did nothing to disrupt the English textile industry because England had other means of obtaining raw cotton, including most notably its plantation holdings in India.

Punch

(November 16)

Artist: Sir John Tenniel

THE WAY THE SOUTHERN NEGROES MET THE YANKEES.

Lor bress you, Massa Dupont, were bin awaitin for you.   Got all de best tings on dat de white man run away and left.   Golly, feel amost good enuff to hug you   Take us right up Norf.

THE WAY THE SOUTHERN NEGROES MET THE YANKEES

⇥ 1861 ⇤

In late 1861, Union Officer Samuel du Pont and the Union navy captured Port Royal, the finest harbor on the Southern coast. After Confederate defenders and white civilians fled the area leaving behind a wealth of land and cotton—and some ten thousand contrabands—du Pont confiscated the land and distributed it to the slaves to work as their own. In this cartoon, the slaves of the "Port Royal Experiment" want to abandon the land they were given for safer haven in the North.

New York Illustrated News
(December 2)
Artist: Thomas Nast

LOOK OUT FOR SQUALLS

⟊═ 1861 ═⟊

Jack Bull scolds a childish, defiant Uncle Sam after the Trent affair. In November 1861, U.S. Captain Charles Wilkes stopped the British steamer *Trent* and arrested C.S.A. diplomats James Mason and John Slidell. Britain considered this move an affront; if Mason and Slidell were not released and an apology from Lincoln was issued, Britain would consider it an act of war. The apology came and Mason and Slidell were released and allowed to continue to England.

Punch

(December 7)

Artist: Sir John Tenniel

LOOK OUT FOR SQUALLS.

Jack Bull. "YOU DO WHAT'S RIGHT, MY SON, OR I'LL BLOW YOU OUT OF THE WATER."

A SHORT BLANKET.

OLD SECESH. "While I cover my Neck, I expose my Feet, and if I cover my Feet, I expose my Neck. Ugh!"

A SHORT BLANKET

⊸⊸ 1861 ⊶⊶

Old Secesh (the Confederacy) lies in bed only partially covered by a blanket labeled "Confederate Army." Old Secesh's exposed shoulder is labeled "VA" for Virginia. "Savannah" is written on one foot and "Charleston" on the other. The Confederate Army consisted of approximately 1,200,000 men as compared to the 2,900,000 men who fought for the Union, and the Confederates could not field an effective response everywhere the Union attacked.

Harper's Weekly
(December 14)
Artist: Frank Bellew

Columbia's Fix

In this year-end cartoon, Columbia, who represents the Union, is pictured here seated on the wall of a harbor fort, pondering her response to the Confederate aggression towards Fort Sumter in Spring 1861.

Punch

(December 28)

Artist: Sir John Tenniel

COLUMBIA'S FIX.

COLUMBIA. "WHICH ANSWER SHALL I SEND?"

1862

KING JEFF THE FIRST. 'Let them Burn! Let the Women and Children Suffer! I'm bound to keep Warm!"

KING JEFF THE FIRST

–=🟰 1862 🟰=–

Part of Charleston burned in an accident unrelated to the war; however, this cartoon symbolizes the sentiment throughout much of the country that Jefferson Davis was a dictator whose concern was not for the citizens of the South, but only for his own aggrandizement.

Harper's Weekly
(January 4)
Signed: J. M. L.

RETROGRESSION
(A VERY SAD PICTURE)

◅══ 1862 ══▻

The cartoonist's use of the word retrogression—return to a primitive state—is probably an allusion to the war and its division of the country. The character in this cartoon likely represents Northern voters who, like those belonging to Tammany Hall, were unwilling to accept a democracy that left them beholden to a South so willing to destoy the Union.

Punch
(February 1)
Artist: Sir John Tenniel

RETROGRESSION (A VERY SAD PICTURE).
War-Dance of the I. O. U. Indian.

GENERAL PILLOW'S RESIGNATION. SKETCHED BY A CORRESPONDENT OF THE MEMPHIS APPEAL See page 206.

GENERAL PILLOW'S RESIGNATION

⊶ 1862 ⊷

During the contest for Tennessee, Confederate General Johnson made a stand at Fort Donelson. Instead of a full force, he sent only 12,000 men under the command of John Floyd, Gideon Pillow, and Simon Buckner. After days of vicious fighting, Floyd and Pillow escaped across the Tennessee River, leaving Buckner to surrender the fort and be taken prisoner. Floyd and Pillow were igno-miniously regarded in the North and South alike for their cowardice.

New York Illustrated News
(February 1)
Artist: probably Thomas Nast

"MASTERLY INACTIVITY," OR SIX MONTHS ON THE POTOMAC.

"MASTERLY INACTIVITY" OR SIX MONTHS ON THE POTOMAC

⇒ 1862 ⇐

Union General George McClellan and Confederate General P. G. T. Beauregard watch each other from opposite sides of the Potomac. Union soldiers offer flowers to Mary Todd Lincoln. Opposite, a Confederate couple is being married by a clergyman. McClellan was well-regarded for his masterly preparations for battle though he feared that his preparations were never enough. Thus, the numer-

ically superior Union army spent the winter of 1861 camped across the Potomac from a smaller and more ill-equipped Confederate army.

Frank Leslie's Illustrated Newspaper
(February 1)
Signed: A. B.

COTTON—A FULL MARKET

COTTON—A SCANT MARKET.

COTTON—A FULL AND SCANT MARKET

⤙ 1862 ⤚

This "before and after" cartoon shows how the scarcity of cotton during the war might affect women's fashions.

Frank Leslie's Illustrated Newspaper
(February 15)
Signed: J. H. H.

FLYING ARTILLERY

⇢➤ 1862 ⟜

General George McClellan was constantly faulted by his government and the northern people for failing to make a decisive move against Richmond in the summer of 1862. The creator of this cartoon obviously thought that McClellan had everything he needed for a successful move against Richmond and jokingly suggests that the U.S. Balloon Corps, used for arial reconnaissance, could help get his troops off the ground.

Frank Leslie's Illustrated Newspaper
(February 22)
Artist unknown

Flying Artillery—a Hint to General McClellan how to "advance on Richmond."

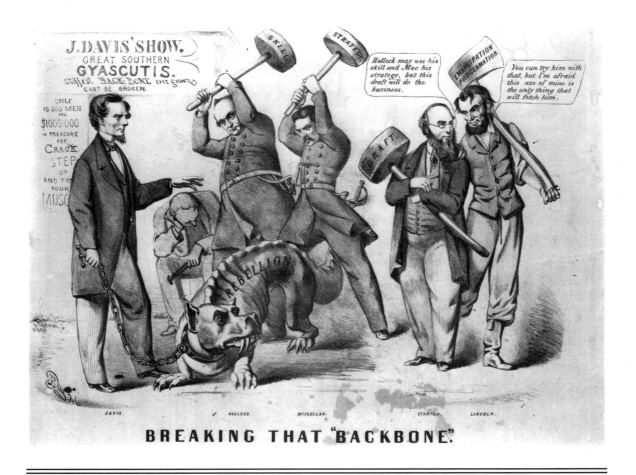

BREAKING THAT "BACKBONE."

BREAKING THAT BACKBONE

⟿ 1862 ⟿

This cartoon addresses Northern efforts to end the war. Jeff Davis displays the "Great Southern Gyascutis," a saber-toothed creature named "Rebellion," advertised as having an unbreakable backbone. Union generals Henry Halleck and George McClellan wield sledgehammers labeled "Skill" and "Strategy." At right, Secretary of War Edwin Stanton holds a hammer labeled "Draft," and Lincoln holds an axe labeled "Emancipation Proclamation." In the background, a man holds a small hammer labeled "Compromise."

Currier & Ives
Artist: Benjamin H. Day

WHISKEY.

THE INAUGURATION AT RICHMOND.

THE INAUGURATION AT RICHMOND

⊷⇒ 1862 ⇐⊶

Jefferson Davis noted the significance of his Presidential inauguration falling on George Washington's birthday because it identified the Confederates with revolutionaries like the founding fathers. Most Northerners, however, saw Davis and Southerners as drunk on power, building the Confederacy on the backs of slaves. Here Davis is pictured as a deathly figure bringing only desolation and suffering to the nation.

Harper's Weekly
(March 15)
Artist unknown

AID AND COMFORT TO THE ENEMY.—THE WAY MR. J. G. B°°°°°T DOES THE LOYAL BUSINESS.

AID AND COMFORT TO THE ENEMY

⊶⇒ 1862 ⇐⊷

During the spring of 1862, while McClellan prepared to move against Richmond, Lee and his forces, including Stonewall Jackson in the Shenandoah Valley, repeatedly outwitted the Union forces as if they knew their plans in advance. This appears to be a reference to what Lincoln and many other critics saw as the northern press working to the disadvantage of the Federal war effort.

New York Illustrated News
(March 22)
Artist: Thomas Nast

REMARKABLE INSTANCE OF VITALITY—THE SMALL END OF THE REBEL ALLIGATOR.

GENERAL McCLELLAN—"*Say, Burnside, I'm hanged if the tail of the reptile don't squirm yet!*"

REMARKABLE INSTANCE OF VITALITY—THE SMALL END OF THE REBEL ALLIGATOR

⟶⚬ 1862 ⚬⟵

This cartoon, in which Union generals have sliced up a huge alligator representing the Confederacy, refers to General Ambrose Burnside's amphibious assault into the North Carolina sounds. With the capture of Fort Macon in April, the Union controlled almost all of the South Carolina coastline, but the Confederates continued to fight on.

Frank Leslie's Illustrated Newspaper
(May 3)
Artist: Frank Bellew

The **Mayor of New Orleans** yielding to "Brute Force."

THE MAYOR OF NEW ORLEANS YIELDING TO "BRUTE FORCE"

→≡ 1862 ≡←

After a brief naval battle, the Union navy easily captured the harbor of the South's largest city, New Orleans, in May 1862, forcing the Confederate forces to abandon the city. During farcical negotiations between the mayor and Union Officer David Farragut, the mayor refused the "honor" of surrendering his city. Two days later, Benjamin Butler and his troops took the city and began a troubled occupation. He later became known as "Beast Butler" for his corrupt tenure as military governor of New Orleans.

Harper's Weekly
(May 17)
Artist: Thomas Nast

THE NEW ORLEANS PLUM

⊷ 1862 ⊶

The capture of New Orleans in May 1862 was a significant victory for the Union. The possession of the port city allowed the Federal navy a convenient base of operations for their forays up the Mississippi River. From February to May, Union forces captured 1,000 miles of navigable rivers, two state capitals, the South's largest city, and a total of 50,000 square miles of territory. These Union victories resulted in a significant decline in Southern morale and a resurgence in Northern spirit.

Punch
(May 24)
Artist: Sir John Tenniel

THE NEW ORLEANS PLUM.

BIG LINCOLN HORNER,
UP IN A CORNER,
THINKING OF HUMBLE PIE;

FOUND UNDER HIS THUMB,
A NEW ORLEANS PLUM,
AND SAID, WHAT A 'CUTE YANKEE AM I!

'EFF DAVIS FALLS BACK ON THE SOUTH PROPER.

JEFF DAVIS—' *Will you allow me to trespass on your hospitality for a short time, till—I can hear from my friends in England: or— procure a small quantity of strychnine."*

JEFF DAVIS FALLS BACK ON THE SOUTH PROPER

⇥⊚ 1862 ⊚⇤

In May of 1862, the Confederacy was in dire straits. It had lost most of the Mississippi valley and McClellan and the Union army were poised outside of Richmond. In this cartoon, Jeff Davis is desperate for help from swamp dwellers, the English, or poison to ease the problems of his exhausted and shoddy troops.

Frank Leslie's Illustrated Newspaper
(May 31)
Artist: Frank Bellew

THE AMERICAN ST. PATRICK DRIVING OUT THE REPTILES.

" And yer won't give up Corcoran, won't yer ?   But I'll make yer, ye spalpeens !   Now take this ! and this ! and this !"

THE AMERICAN ST. PATRICK
DRIVING OUT THE REPTILES

⇒ 1862 ⇐

In 1861, Walter Smith, captain of the Confederate schooner, *The Enchantress,* was captured, tried, and convicted of piracy. In retaliation, Confederate Secretary of War Judah Benjamin ordered that Colonel Michael Corcoran, an Irishman who led the 69th New York Militia at the first battle of Bull Run where he was captured, be held as a hostage unless the Union released Smith. Smith's conviction was overturned in 1862, and Corcoran was exchanged and later made brigadier general retroactive to the date of his capture.

Frank Leslie's Illustrated Newspaper
(July 5)
Artist unknown

THE LATEST FROM AMERICA;

Or, the New York "Eye-Duster," to be taken Every Day.

⇥⊱ 1862 ⊰⇤

Throughout much of the war, the northern press criticized Lincoln and his generals' waging of the war. This image of victory being turned into defeat by the New York press is likely a reference to the newspaper coverage of the battle of Shiloh in May 1862. Though Grant snatched victory from the jaws of defeat, most reports focused on the jaws, vividly recounting stories of Federal soldiers massacred by the Confederate army and false accusations that Grant was drunk during the battle.

Punch
(July 26)
Artist: Sir John Tenniel

PERIODICAL SCARE OF THE OLD PARTY AT THE WAR DEPARTMENT.

PERIODICAL SCARE OF THE OLD PARTY AT THE WAR DEPARTMENT

⇒ 1862 ⇐

Just when it seemed the United States could end the war, Stonewall Jackson's forces staged a successful run in the Shenandoah Valley, defeating Irvin McDowell's corps who were on their way to reinforce McClellan outside of Richmond and help capture the Confederate capital. Until his death, Jackson's victories in the Valley were a continual thorn in the side of Union forces. In this cartoon, Union Secretary of War Edwin Stanton is taken aback by a Jackson "jack-in-the-box."

New York Illustrated News
(August 9)
Artist unknown

LINCOLN'S TWO DIFFICULTIES.

Lin. "WHAT? NO MONEY! NO MEN!"

LINCOLN'S TWO DIFFICULTIES

⟶ 1862 ⟵

In the early years of the war, there was no taxation system in place that would allow Lincoln to pay for troops and military supplies. The government was forced to rely on loans from banks to make their payments. After the Union defeat at Bull Run, McClellan's failure to attack Richmond, and the threat of a war with England over the seizure of Mason and Slidell from the *Trent*, Northern banks suspended their government loans, leaving Lincoln with no way to pay soldiers, suppliers, or contractors.

Punch
(August 23)
Artist: Sir John Tenniel

FEDERAL GENERALS ON THE LOOKOUT FOR "STONEWALL," JACKSON.

FEDERAL GENERALS ON THE LOOKOUT FOR "STONEWALL" JACKSON

⊷⊷ 1862 ⊷⊷

After destroying Federal supplies at Manassas Junction, Stonewall Jackson and his men lay in wait for General John Pope's troops on the old battle-field of Bull Run. Pope exhausted his infantry looking for Jackson and when they finally found and fought Jackson's troops, Pope thought the victory was his. Lee and Longstreet finally joined Jackson and pum-melled Pope's army. Both sides suf-fered heavy casualties but the Confederates won a sure victory.

New York Illustrated News
(September 13)
Artist unknown

ENTHUSIASTIC RECEPTION IN MARYLAND OF THE AUTHOR OF THOSE AFFECTING LINES, "MY MARYLAND."

ARISE, ARISE MY MARYLAND

⊷⊷ 1862 ⊷⊷

As a border state, Maryland was home to both Confederates and Unionists. Throughout the early part of the war, Confederate officials were confident that upon the arrival of the Southern army in Maryland, thousands of Marylanders would rise up and join in the fight against the Union army. But in September 1862, when Confederate soldiers entered Frederick, Maryland, singing "Maryland, My Maryland" they received a less than enthusiastic welcome.

The New York Illustrated News
(October 11)
Artist unknown

ABE LINCOLN'S LAST CARD: OR, ROUGE-ET-NOIR.

ABE LINCOLN'S LAST CARD OR
THE ROUGE-ET-NOIR

⇒⊨ 1862 ⊨⇐

After the Union stopped Lee's advance in the Antietam campaign in September 1862, Lincoln issued a preliminary edict on emancipation. In this cartoon, he is about to play the race card in a game conducted over a powder keg.

Punch
(October 18)
Artist: Sir John Tenniel

A LUCKY COINCIDENCE—FAST DAY IN RICHMOND.

DINAH—" *Oh, massa, so berry lucky; jist as I get down to market and find dere's nothing to sell and nothing to eat, out comes Mister Davis's proclamation for a Fast Day. Ain't it real first-rate?*"
[Hungry F. F. V. don't see it, but can't help it.]

In the fall of 1862, food was scarce in Richmond. The fighting had taken a toll on the land, farmers were away at war, people had to share food with the army, and the harvest was especially small. Government declarations of fasting and prayer were often ridiculed as in this cartoon.

Frank Leslie's Illustrated Newspaper
(October 25)
Artist: Thomas Nast

MASKS AND FACES

⟜ 1862 ⟝

In this pro-Southern cartoon, Lincoln takes off his mask to reveal his true persona: Satan. His evil deed, the Emancipation Proclamation, lies on the ground in front of him and is dated January 1, 1863. In the background is the unfinished Washington Monument representing the Southern belief that the forefathers had fought for rights that included slavery.

Southern Illustrated News

(November 8)

Artist unknown

MASKS AND FACES.

King Abraham before and after issuing the EMANCIPATION PROCLAMATION.

GRAND SET-TO AT COOPER INSTITUTE BETWEEN GEN CASSIUS M. CLAY, ALIAS THE "RUSSIAN SLOGGER," AND GEORGE FRANCIS TRAIN, ALIAS THE "BOSTON PET." FROM A SKETCH BY OUR COMIC SPECIAL.

GRAND SET-TO AT COOPER INSTITUTE

⇒ 1862 ⇐

Union General Cassius Clay, a lawyer, politician, and ardent abolitionist from Kentucky, was appointed U.S. minister to Russia in 1861. He resigned his post to accept a commission in the U.S. army volunteers. After returning from Russia, however, he announced that he would not fight so long as slavery was protected in the Southern states. George Francis Train, a Boston Merchant, was an outspoken pro-Union orator. This cartoon alludes to the inherent differences between Clay's resignation over abolition and Train's ardently pro-Union stance.

New York Illustrated News
(November 22)
Artist unknown

1863

THIS IS OLD MOTHER LINCOLN EXPLAINING TO OLD MOTHER STANTON HOW THE SLAUGHTER OF OUR
TROOPS AT FREDERICKSBURG REMINDS HIM OF AN ANECDOTE HE HEARD OUT WEST.

OLD MOTHER LINCOLN AND
OLD MOTHER STATON

⇢⇥ 1863 ⇤⇠

In December 1862, the Union sustained a devastating loss to the Confederacy at Fredericksburg, Maryland, due largely to mismanagement by commanding officers. The Union lost nearly 13,000 soldiers while the Confederacy suffered only about 5,000 wounded or dead. Though the commanding general, Ambrose Burnside, took much of the blame upon himself, the president and his secretary of war were also targets for Northerners' frustration with the war effort.

The New York Illustrated News
(January 10)
Artist unknown

ANY MORE SCRUBBING TO GIVE OUT?

⌐═ 1863 ═⌐

Benjamin Butler conquered New Orleans in May 1862, and became a harsh military governor there. When a man sympatic to the Confederacy took down a Union flag, Butler had him hanged. Confederate officers and activists were rounded up and either jailed or banished from the city. Butler was removed from his command in New Orleans in December 1862. Eventually he took over the Department of Virginia and North Carolina, later known as the Army of the James.

Harper's Weekly

(January 17)

Signed: J. M. L.

Uncle Abe. "Hello! Ben, is that you? Glad to see you!"
Butler. "Yes, Uncle Abe. Got through with that New Orleans Job. Cleaned them out and scrubbed them up! *Any more scrubbing to give out?*"

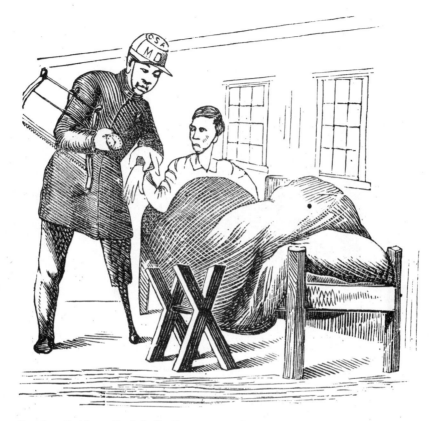

Scene in a Confederate Hospital—For the benefit of some of our "M. D.'s," which can be explained by any brave soldier with an "empty sleeve," or who perambulates the streets with a wooden leg.

SCENE IN A CONFEDERATE HOSPITAL

⇀⇒ 1863 ⇐↼

In this poorly drawn cartoon criticizing the frequency with which men's limbs were amputated, a doctor for the Confederate States of America takes the pulse of a bedridden soldier who has no legs. A saw horse rests beside the bed. The doctor carries a saw under one arm and he, himself, has a wooden leg.

Southern Illustrated News
(January 24)
Artist unknown

SCHOOLMASTER LINCOLN AND HIS BOYS.—*Lincoln*—Waal, boys, what's the matter with yer; you haint been hurt, hev yer? *McClellan.*—Them fellers that run away has been beatin' us. *Lincoln.*—What fellers? *McClellan.*—Bob Lee and Jeb Stuart and them. *Lincoln.*—I sent you out to fetch them same fellers back, so's I could wallop 'em. *McClellan.*—Yes, but Bob Lee took and bunged me in the eye. *Pope.*—And Stunwall Jackson he kicked me in the rear until he broke my arm. *Banks.*—Yes, and that same feller gouged me and run me until I run my leg off and hev to wear a wooden one. *Burnside.*—All of 'em, Bob Lee, Stunwall and Stuart, jumped on me at Fredericksburg and give me fits; that's the reason my jaw is tied up, to keep my teeth from chatterin', for I've had a fit of the ager ever since. *Lincoln.*—You are a worthless set, all of you. You haint no spunk. I'm agoin' to spank every one of yer. Come up here.

SCHOOLMASTER LINCOLN AND HIS BOYS

⟶ 1863 ⟵

In this crudely drawn cartoon, Lincoln is again a schoolmaster. Here he shakes a ruler labeled "Constitution" at four bandaged students, George McClellan, John Pope, Nathaniel Banks, and Ambrose Burnside, all generals defeated by Confederate troops.

Southern Illustrated News
(January 31)
Artist unknown

SHAMEFUL EXTORTION! *Colored Lady* (loq.)—What! dollar and half for dis ninepence Cali-
ker, an' ole fashion at dat. Great King!

SHAMEFUL EXTORTION!

➤ 1863 ◆

During the war, Southerners had to do without goods previously supplied by the North. War profiteers and blockade runners smuggled goods into the Confederate States; however, few people could afford the inflated prices. This cartoon might also suggest that former slaves would be unable to survive without their masters to provide for them.

Southern Illustrated News
(February 14)
Artist unknown

MASTER ABRAHAM LINCOLN GETS A NEW TOY.

MASTER ABRAHAM LINCOLN GETS A NEW TOY

⊷≋ 1863 ≋⊷

A childlike Lincoln is shown playing "war" with his puppets. He manipulates Joseph "Fighting Joe" Hooker, while other Union Generals lie discarded on the shelf. The Emancipation Proclamation on the back wall may mock the shrewdness of Lincoln's proclamation, which changed the war from a fight to preserve the Union to a crusade to free the slaves.

Southern Illustrated News

(February 28)

Artist unknown

THE COPPERHEAD PARTY.——IN FAVOR OF *A VIGOROUS PROSECUTION OF PEACE!*

THE COPPERHEAD PARTY

⇾⇾ 1863 ⇽⇽

Copperheads, or Peace Democrats, were Northern Democrats who opposed the war. In this cartoon, three copperheads look angrily at Columbia who carries a sword and a shield.

Harper's Weekly

(February 28)

Artist unknown

DON QUIXOTE AND SANCHO PANZA

⟨⟩ 1863 ⟨⟩

Lincoln, dressed in armor, is portrayed as the deluded idealist Don Quixote, while General Benjamin Butler, carrying a whiskey jug, is his faithful squire Sancho Panza. A windmill in the background signifies the futility of the men's mission.

Confederate War Etchings
Artist: V. Blada (Adalbert Johann Volck)

THE FOOD QUESTION DOWN SOUTH.

JEFF DAVIS. "See! see! the beautiful Boots just come to me from the dear ladies of Baltimore!"

BEAUREGARD. "Ha! Boots? Boots? When shall we eat them? Now?"

THE FOOD QUESTION DOWN SOUTH

⟫ 1863 ⟪

Throughout the war, the South experienced problems with the supply and transportation of food and other necessities to Confederate troops as well as to the populace. In 1863, hamlets and towns across the Confederacy including most notably, the Confederate capital of Richmond, were the scenes of bread riots by desperate women and children.

Harper's Weekly
(May 9)
Artist unknown

THE LITTLE JOKER.

CHORUS (Greeley, Bennett, Raymond)—"*Know where it is—under that middle hat, of course ; under Keyes.*"

THE LITTLE JOKER

⤖ 1863 ⤔

This cartoon alludes to the quandary facing Lincoln and the Union about how to win the war. In 1863 Union General Joseph Hooker commanded the Army of the Potomac with Union General Erasmus Keyes. They were instrumental in defending Washington and Baltimore against Lee's army during the Gettysburg campaign. The reference to Davis and the city of Richmond alludes to the attempts of the U.S. Army of Virginia to capture Richmond. There is a subtle reference to the Northern press's criticisms of the Federal war effort.

Frank Leslie's Illustrated Newspaper
(June 27)
Artist unknown

JEFF DAVIS'S FACE, as seen through South Mountain Gap, FOURTH OF JULY, 1863.

JEFF DAVIS'S FACE AS SEEN THROUGH SOUTH MOUNTAIN GAP

⇒ 1863 ⇐

After Lee's loss at Gettysburg in July 1863, and his retreat back across the Potomac, Richmond and the Confederate government once again became a target for Union attack. Davis is pictured here peering through South Mountain Gap in Maryland at his army's loss in Pennsylvania.

Harper's Weekly
(July 18)
Artist unknown

The President's Order No. 252

◦═══ 1863 ═══◦

After the Emancipation Proclamation and the full-scale recruitment of black troops, the Confederacy threatened to execute captured black soldiers, treating them as fugitive slaves rather than as prisoners of war. Although this policy was never officially carried out, Lincoln and the United States threatened "appropriate" reprisals against Confederate P.O.Ws.

Harper's Weekly
(August 15)
Artist unknown

THE PRESIDENT'S ORDER No. 252.

Mr. Lincoln. "Look here, Jeff. Davis! if you lay a finger on that boy, to hurt him, I'll lick this *Ugly Cub of yours* within an inch of his life!"

THE NAUGHTY BOY GOTHAM, WHO WOULD NOT TAKE THE DRAFT.

THE NAUGHTY BOY GOTHAM, WHO WOULD NOT TAKE THE DRAFT

◦═ 1863 ═◦

In July 1862, Congress passed a law authorizing a military draft in Northern states that did not meet their quota of troops voluntarily. This met with violent resistance in Pennsylvania, Ohio, Indiana, and Wisconsin. To quell the disturbances and enforce the draft, the War Department sent troops to arrest and imprison hundreds of men, mostly Democrats. In 1863, New York City, with its large Irish population and powerful Democratic machine, also erupted in violence lasting four days and killing at least 105 people. Again troops were sent in to quell the violence.

Frank Leslie's Illustrated Newspaper
(*August 29*)
Artist unknown

This colored person is NOT engaged in the capture of conscripts, as will doubtless be asserted by certain Yankee prisoners who witness the operation from the windows of the "Libby," when they return North.

THIS COLORED PERSON IS NOT ENGAGED IN THE CAPTURE OF CONSCRIPTS

⤖ 1863 ⬅

In April of 1862, the Confederate Congress passed the first conscription act, or military draft, that North America had ever seen. The idea of conscription was at odds with Southern notions of individual liberty, and many Southerners evaded the draft. In this cartoon, a man tries to catch a fleeing dog. In the background is Libby Prison in Richmond, Virginia.

Southern Illustrated News
(September 12)
Signed: Hurdle

RECIPE TO GET RID OF EXTORTIONERS —Chain them to a stake, as above; pile their ill-gotten gains around them, and any passer-by will fire the mass. This will have the happy effect, both of ridding the community of their presence, and at the same time reducing the circulating medium.

RECIPE TO GET RID OF EXTORTIONERS

⋙ 1863 ⋘

The South printed paper money to finance the war, which led to severe inflation. One suggestion to improve the value of the dollar was to remove as much as two-thirds of paper money from circulation by offering to exchange it for interest-bearing bonds. This cartoon suggests another way to remove some of the undervalued Confederate currency along with extortioners.

Southern Illustrated News

(September 19)

Signed: H.A.

Office Board of Examiners—Examination of a Conscript.

DEDICATED ONLY TO SUCH INCOMPETENT OR PERVERSE M. S. AS THOSE WHO INSIST UPON BURDENING THE ARMY AND HOSPITALS WITH MEN NOTORIOUSLY UNFIT FOR DUTY. MANY A HUMANE AND SKILLFUL M. S. THROUGHOUT THE COUNTRY WILL APPRECIATE THE RIGHTEOUS HIT.

Office Board of Examiners—Examination of a Conscript

1863

Confederate soldiers enlisted for one year when the war began and by spring 1862, the Confederate Army was in danger of collapsing. Later, the Conscription Act called to service all men between the ages of 18 and 35 and also allowed drafted men to pay substitutes to take their places. Many were physically or mentally unsuitable. In this cartoon, two Confederate medical department officers, depicted as jackasses, happily examine a physically unfit conscript. In the background is a well-stocked bar.

Southern Punch

(October 10)

Artist unknown

CONTRAST.

CONFEDERATE PRISONER,
OHIO PENITENTIARY.

FEDERAL PRISONERS,
BELLE ISLE.

CONTRAST OF PRISONS

⇢⇒ 1863 ⇐⇠

The practice of the North and South exchanging prisoners collapsed in 1863. When Grant took control of the Union army, he argued that to repatriate prisoners would only strengthen the South. This cartoon contrasts the solitary confinement of a Confederate prisoner with the "good" life (including tobacco) of Federal prisoners. Prison conditions in both the North and the South were ghastly. Men died in droves of starvation and disease. Approximately 30,000 Union soldiers and 26,000 Confederate soldiers died in prisons.

Southern Illustrated News
(October 10)
Signed: Hurdle

THANKSGIVING TABLE

A BAD EGG FOR JEFF DAVIS—CHATTANOOGA.

A Bad Egg for Jeff Davis— Chattanooga

⇥ 1863 ⇤

Tennessee, a border state like Maryland, was a hotly contested battlefield in the western theater during the first three years of the war. The fall of Chattanooga to General Ulysses S. Grant's army in November 1863, signaled the loss of Tennessee to the Confederacy forever.

New York Illustrated News
(October 17)
Artist unknown

GREAT AMERICAN TRAGEDIANS, COMEDIANS,
CLOWNS AND ROPE DANZERS IN
THEIR FAVORITE CHARACTERS.

Your honours players ...are come to play a pleasant comedy.... Is it a
Comedy....a Christmas Gambol or a tumbling trick.....No my Lord it
is   more pleasing stuff.... it is a kind of history.

JESTER LINCOLN AND HIS PUPPETS

⟿ 1863 ⟾

A skeleton lifts the curtain on Lincoln and his puppets in this cartoon that mocks Lincoln and his handling of the war. Lincoln is portrayed as a jester. Salmon Chase, Secretary of the Treasury, sits behind the box office window. Simon Cameron, Secretary of War, hangs from a string; Secretary of the Navy Gideon Welles sits in a row boat; General Benjamin Butler slumps nearby; General John Frémont is on horseback; General Winfield Scott is in a wheelchair; and General George McClellan rides a hobby horse.

Confederate War Etchings
Artist: V. Blada (Adalbert Johann Volck)

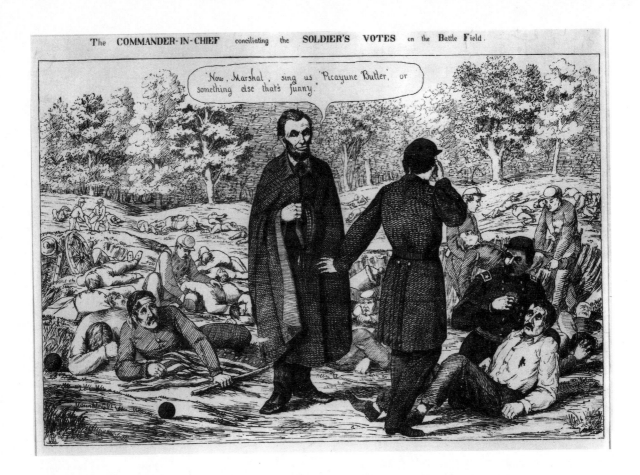

THE COMMANDER-IN-CHIEF CONCILIATING THE SOLDIER'S VOTES ON THE BATTLE FIELD

⇒ 1863 ⇐

In this dark anti-Lincoln cartoon, the president walks among the wounded and the dead on the battlefield looking for votes. He asks his friend Marshal Lamon to "sing us 'Picayune Butler' or something else that's funny." This is a reference to incorrect reports in the *New York World* that Lincoln joked while touring the battlefield of Antietam. Note that Lincoln holds a plaid Scotch cap and wears a large overcoat, signifiers of his cowardice.

Printer unknown
Signed: C. A. L.

WRITING THE EMANCIPATION PROCLAMATION

⇒ 1863 ⇐

Lincoln writes the Emancipation Proclamation surrounded by Satanic symbols. He rests his left foot atop the U.S. Constitution. His inkwell is held by a demon. The table has hooved feet and the corners are buttressed by horned heads of African Americans. On the wall behind him, hangs a painting of John Brown and a painting of a slave revolt.

Confederate War Etchings
Artist: V. Blada (Adalbert Johann Volck)

ROSECRANZ'S ADDRESS TO HIS SOLDIERS:

"We have fought the Battle of Chickamauga to gain our position at Chattanooga, AND HERE WE ARE!!!"

CAUSE OF ROSECRANZ'S SUPERCEDURE!

⟶ 1863 ⟵

Union General William Starke Rosecranz hoped to take Chattanooga and occupy Knoxville and eastern Tennessee; however, Confederate General James Longstreet and his army joined General Braxton Bragg's army at Chickamauga where they defeated Rosecranz's Army of the Cumberland and drove them back to Chattanooga. The loss of this battle ended Rosecranz's career as a field commander.

Southern Illustrated News
(November 7)
Signed: Z. C.

Abduction of the Yankee Goddess of Liberty.

THE PRINCE OF DARKNESS (ABRAHAM LINCOLN) BEARS
HER AWAY TO HIS INFERNAL REGIONS.

GODDESS—Monster of Perdition, let me go !

ABRAHAM—Never ! You have been preaching about the Constitution too long already. I was the first to rebel against constituted
authority. "Hell is murky !" You go thither !

ABDUCTION OF THE YANKEE GODDESS OF LIBERTY

⊸≡◉ 1863 ◉≡⊷

Lincoln, again depicted as Satan, takes Liberty to hell and tells her of his disdain for "constituted authority." This cartoon is another allusion to the Southern belief that their fight paralleled the founding fathers' fight for liberty and that the Constitution protected slavery.

Southern Punch
(November 14)
Artist unknown

1864

THE TRUE PEACE COMMISSIONERS.

Published by Currier & Ives, 152 Nassau St N.Y.

THE TRUE PEACE COMMISSIONERS

⇢ 1864 ⇠

Four union officers (from left to right Philip Sheridan, Ulysses S. Grant, David Farragut, and William Tecumseh Sherman) threaten Robert E. Lee and Jefferson Davis and demand that they surrender to the United States. Lee replies that he will not surrender but will suggest an armistice through the Chicago platform in the upcoming presidential election. This attempt at peace was seen as a strategic move and, as evidenced by Davis's comment, not a true attempt to end the war.

Currier & Ives
Artist: probably John Cameron

Lincoln and Seward Watching over the Drooping Eagle.

ABE.—I guess that fowl is pretty well tired up. I calculate he's going to cave in.

SEWARD.—He certainly looks a little shaky at present but I see no harm yet—simply moulting Sir, that's all—a black draught will put him all right, Sir. In thirty days that bird Sir, will be in better plumage than ever.

ABE.—Well. I hope so, but I think doctor the *black draughts* already given have pretty well played the devil with him.

LINCOLN AND SEWARD WATCHING OVER THE DROOPING EAGLE

⚬ 1864 ⚬

Union Secretary of State William Henry Seward sits with Lincoln as he worries over a sickly bald eagle. Seward suggests that a black draught will cure him, but Lincoln is not so sure. The play on the word draught, refers to the decision by both the South and North to employ African Americans in the army. The Confederate Congress authorized the use of 20,000 black Confederates as cooks and laborers, while approximately 180,000 black men joined the Union Army.

Southern Punch
(January 2)
Artist unknown

THE LOGIC OF EXTORTION.

GROCER, (*to indignant customer,*)—*No'm; we couldn't sell this sugar for less than four dollars a pound. You see we have to pay the marketmen twenty-five dollars a bushel for potatoes, &c., &c., &c.*

MARKETMAN—*Yes'm; I has to charge twenty-five dollars a bushel for them potatoes; I has to pay four dollars a pound for every pound of sugar I gets, &c., &c., &c.*

THE LOGIC OF EXTORTION

⊷≡ 1864 ≡⊶

Farmers in the South had to shift their focus to producing food instead of cotton and tobacco during the war, but because of inadequate trans-portation and distribution channels, people went hungry. Food shortages, combined with inflation and high prices, meant many civilians, as well as soldiers, went without sustenance. Many marketmen and others involved in the control of food sup-plies were seen as corrupt, profiting from the war while Southern citizens suffered.

Southern Illustrated News
(January 2)
Artist unknown

COLD COMFORT

⊷⊷ 1864 ⊷⊷

In 1864, the South was suffering from out-of-control
inflation, food and textile
shortages, and low morale,
despite the European views
to the contrary. In this cartoon, Confederate president
Jeff Davis reads a letter
from the Pope and com-
ments that he'd rather have
clothing and food than a
flattering greeting.

Harper's Weekly
(January 30)
Artist unknown

COLD COMFORT.

JEFF DAVIS (*reading the Pope's Letter*). "Well, it's very good of His Holiness to call
me 'Illustrious President,' and all that, but it would have been more to the purpose if he
had sent me a lot of his cast-off clothes and some broken victuals!"

Chairman of Committee on "Subsistence."

Chairman of Committee on "Subsistence"

⇥ 1864 ⇤

This cartoon drives home the fact that those with money and power rarely go hungry. Mainly, though, it points to people's frustrations with the inadequate food supply and with war profiteering. Confederate supply agents were not always able to find, pay for, and transport food to citizens.

Southern Punch
(January 30)
Artist unknown

A HARD CASE.

MISS SUSAN, *despairingly*—"There! it's no use, Kitty; you can go and take the old thing off. Was there ever such barbarity? Who but the Yankees would ever have thought of making hoop skirts contraband of war?"

A HARD CASE

⇢═ 1864 ═⇠

Morale was low among Southern women late in the war because of the multiple hardships they had endured. In this cartoon, a white Southern woman despairs at having to make or repair a hoop skirt and at the impossibility of getting a new one because of the war. The stance of the slave girl being used as a clothes hanger underscores an unintended irony of the woman's lament, "Was there ever such barbarity?"

Southern Illustrated News
(February 6)
Artist unknown

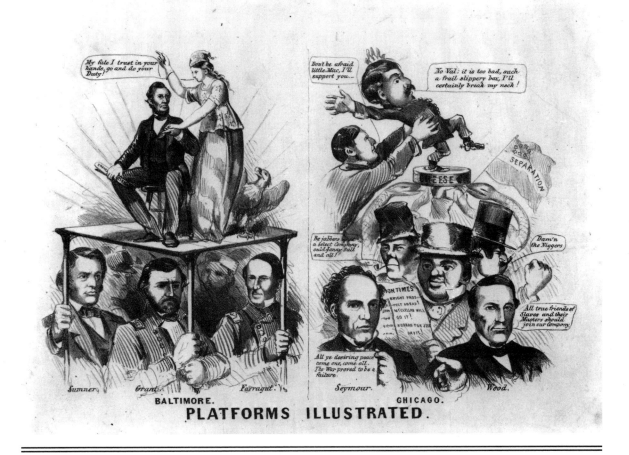

PLATFORMS ILLUSTRATED.

PLATFORMS ILLUSTRATED

⟶ 1864 ⟵

The 1864 presidential conventions inspired this pro-Republican cartoon. Lincoln holds the Emancipation Proclamation (left) and is encouraged by Liberty to carry on, supported by Massachusetts senator Charles Sumner, Union General Ulysses S. Grant, and Union Admiral David Farragut. The Democratic platform (right) has the look of a sideshow, with a tiny George McClellan being hoisted atop a cheese box by Copperhead (Peace Democrat) leader Clement Vallandigham. John Bull (center) reads a pro-McClellan issue of the *London Times*.

Prang & Company
Artist unknown

RECURITING

===== 1864 =====

With the end of the war imminent, Northern capital-ists quickly saw the eco-nomic benefits of recruiting black men for the menial jobs that white workers tra-ditionally refused. Similarly, the U.S. government took advantage of African American hopes for a better life by recruiting them as soldiers. Only rarely did such soldiers enjoy duties extending beyond manual labor; the Massachusetts 54th, led by Robert Gould Shaw, being the most signif-icant exception.

Frank Leslie's Illustrated Newspaper
(February 13)
Signed: W. P.

RECRUITING.

1ST BROKER—" *Now, then, yer know I spoke to yer first.*"
2ND DITTO—" *Can't you let the gentleman decide for himself.*"
BEWILDERED MAN AND BROTHER—" *You bofe very kind gemmin, but I'se afraid dey's waiting up dere for me to finish up dat whitewashin'.*"

"I WISH I WAS IN DIXIE!"

PLAINTIVE AIR—Sung nightly in Washington by that Celebrated Delineator, ABRAHAM LINCOLN.

"I WISH I WAS IN DIXIE"

⇒ 1864 ⇐

This cartoon mocks Lincoln and the Union belief that if Richmond were captured the war would end. Lincoln plays a banjo in front of a map of Richmond and sings, "I wish I was in Dixie." A pardon for political offenses sticks out of his pocket. Tools associated with his railsplitting days are also pictured.

Southern Illustrated News
(February 27)
Artist unknown

THE FURLOUGH SOUTH

~⊂◦⊃~ 1864 ~⊂◦⊃~

Throughout the war, Northern officials and citizens alike derided Southern women for their ardent support of the Confederate "cause," calling them "firebrands" and "Southern spitfires" and blaming them for the long duration of the war.

Frank Leslie's Illustrated Newspaper
(March 19)
Artist unknown

THE FURLOUGH SOUTH.

Rebel returns to the bosom of his family. Being clad in the stolen uniform of one of our gallant defenders, he is mistaken by his wife for a " Yank" and received accordingly.

AN EXPEDITION IN PURSUIT OF LIVE·STOCK.

No. 1.

A Flank Movement Planned.

No. 2.

Failure of the Expedition.

An Expedition in Pursuit of Live Stock

⊷≋ 1864 ≋⊶

Food for soldiers was scarce and their diet monotonous, and because of transportation difficulties, Confederate soldiers sometimes went for several days without rations. To supplement their limited provisions, soldiers stole pigs and chickens from farms and hunted for wild game. This cartoon compares the capture of a frog to a military operation.

Southern Illustrated News
(April 23)
Artist unknown

BUTLER, THE BEAST, AT WORK.

BUTLER, THE BEAST, AT WORK

⊷══ 1864 ══⊷

Late in 1863, Union General Benjamin Butler took command of the military departments of Virginia and North Carolina. In this cartoon he is shown as a jackal digging up the grave of Albert Sidney Johnston, a Confederate general killed on the first day of fighting at Shiloh in 1862.

Southern Illustrated News
(April 30)
Artist unknown

HOSPITABLE INVITATION.

Soldier, (to town friend who has run up to camp to see the boys,)—You had just as well stay with us, to-night, old fellow, and go down on the morning train—get to town too late this afternoon to do anything.

Gent.—Ah! hem, thank you—believe I must go down—besides, don't like to crowd you.

HOSPITABLE INVITATION

◦━ 1864 ━◦

This cartoon makes fun of men who are not engaged in the war effort and suggests that they are cowards. In this cartoon, a visitor to a Confederate encampment is eager to get back to the safety and comfort of town life.

Southern Illustrated News
(May 14)
Signed: Casey

GRANT TURNING LEE'S FLANK.

GRANT TURNING LEE'S FLANK

⁓ 1864 ⁓

In the summer of 1864, Federal Commander Ulysses S. Grant turned the tide of the war against Lee, chasing the Confederate army out of Richmond and eventually laying siege to Petersburg. In the end, Grant's maneuvers and refusal to retreat regardless of the casualty toll resulted in the end of the war and Union victory.

Harper's Weekly
(June 11)
Artist unknown

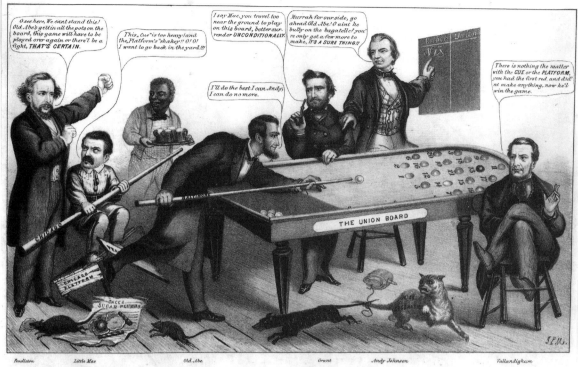

A LITTLE GAME OF BAGATELLE, BETWEEN OLD ABE THE RAIL SPLITTER & LITTLE MAC THE GUNBOAT GENERAL.

Published by J.L.Magee , South East cor. Third & Dock Sts. Philad.ª

A LITTLE GAME OF BAGATELLE BETWEEN OLD ABE THE RAIL SPLITTER AND LITTLE MAC THE GUNBOAT GENERAL

⇜ 1864 ⇝

This election-year cartoon pits Democrat George McClellan against Republican incumbent Abraham Lincoln in a game of bagatelle. Lincoln's running mate, Andrew Johnson, keeps score on a board that reflects that the Coppers (Copperheads) have "Nix." To the left of McClellan is his running mate George Pendleton. Copperhead leader Clement Vallandigham sits at the far right. Union general Ulysses S. Grant smokes a pipe at the edge of the table.

John L. Magee, printer
Artist: John L. Magee

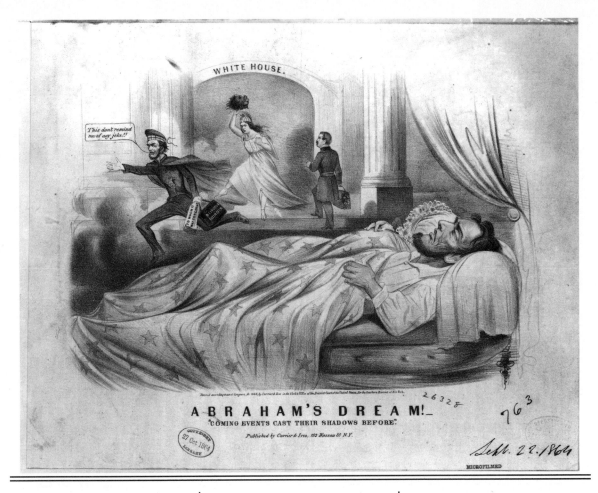

ABRAHAM'S DREAM!

⇌ 1864 ⇌

Lincoln dreams that he is defeated in the 1864 election. Columbia stands before the White House holding the head of a black man and kicking Lincoln away. Lincoln, dressed in a Scotch cap and long cape, is hurriedly returning to Illinois. On the right, McClellan climbs the steps to the White House.

Currier & Ives
Artist: probably Louis Maurer

PATRIOTIC YOUNG LADY—"*Never mind your ankles, Jennie; we had better go with short skirts than our brave soldiers want bandages.*"

RISING HEMLINES OF PATRIOTIC YOUNG LADIES

⤙══ 1864 ══⤚

During the war, the U.S. government created the U.S. Sanitary Commission. The Commission's official powers were only investigatory and advisory, but its structure offered countless Northern women an opportunity to contribute to the war effort, many by volunteering as nurses. This cartoon celebrates not only Northern women's aid for U.S. soldiers, but also notes the necessity of relaxing normal ideals of proper behavior in times of war.

Frank Leslie's Illustrated News
(July 9)
Artist unknown

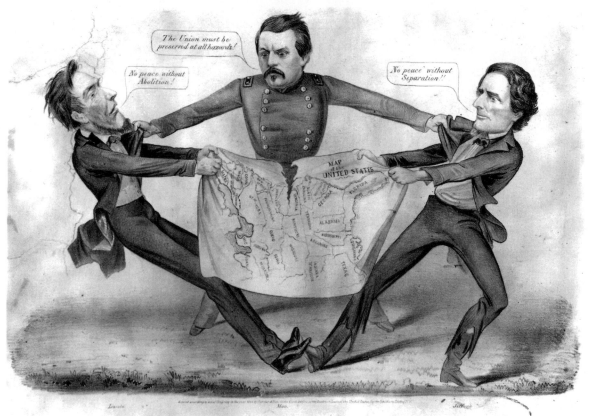

THE TRUE ISSUE OR "THATS WHATS THE MATTER".

THE TRUE ISSUE OR "THATS WHATS THE MATTER"

⇥ 1864 ⇤

Democratic presidential candidate George McClellan intercedes between Lincoln and Jeff Davis who are in a tug-of-war using a map of the United States. Part of the Democratic platform called for the immediate end to fighting, but personally McClellan supported the war.

Currier & Ives
Artist unknown

PEACE MOVEMENT NORTH!

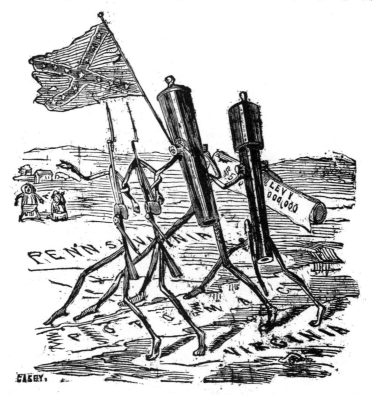

Our Commissioners cross the Border, prepared for Negotiation.

PEACE MOVEMENT NORTH!

→ 1864 ←

The South wanted peace, but they wanted it through victory. An armistice was considered by many to be akin to treason. In this cartoon, the weapons of war cross the Potomac to talk with the North.

Southern Illustrated News
(August 20)
Signed: Casey

THIS REMINDS ME OF A LITTLE JOKE

⇢═ 1864 ═⇠

Cartoonists usually used Lincoln's habit of telling humorous stories to make him look silly, but in this cartoon, published close to the election, McClellan is portrayed as the joke.

Harper's Weekly
(September 17)
Artist unknown

THE AMERICAN ICONOCLAST.
GENERAL GRANT BREAKING THE GOLDEN CALF.

THE AMERICAN ICONOCLAST

→⇒ 1864 ⇐←

Probably a reference to Ulysses S. Grant's pursuit of Lee outside of Richmond after a Federal victory, rather than U.S. Generals' traditional refusal to give chase. The use of a biblical reference to the worship of a golden calf points to the worship of military text-book maneuvers by Lincoln's previous generals.

Frank Leslie's Illustrated Newspaper
(October 15)
Artist unknown

ACROBATIC NOVELTIES.

A DIFFICULT TRICK (WALKING ON A LONG AND A SHORT STILT) NOW IN REHEARSAL BY PROFESSOR GEORGE B. M'CLELLAN. ALSO THE ONE STILT PERFORMANCE OF THE EXPERT PENDLETON.

ACROBATIC NOVELTIES

⇜ 1864 ⇝

This pre-election cartoon highlights the tricky position McClellan was in as the Democratic Presidential nominee. He tries to balance on a short stilt labeled "peace" and on a longer one labeled "war." The party platform called for an end to the fighting, but McClellan supported the war. His running mate, George Pendleton, a friend of Copperhead leader Clement Vallandigham, balances on one stilt, presumably peace, in the background.

Frank Leslie's Illustrated Newspaper
(October 29)
Artist: Frank Bellew

"I KNEW HIM, HORATIO; A FELLOW OF INFINITE JEST. * * * WHERE BE YOUR GIBES NOW?—*Hamlet, Act IV., Scene* 1.

"I Knew Him, Horatio; A Fellow of Infinite Jest"

1864

McClellan, dressed as Hamlet, stands near an open grave and holds the head of Abraham Lincoln. He speaks Hamlet's lines about Yorick, the King's jester, whose skull Hamlet came upon in a graveyard: "A fellow of infinite jest . . . where be your gibes now?" The cartoon appeared after a false story published in the *New York World* claimed that Lincoln was telling jokes while touring Antietam. At right is Horatio Seymour, governor of New York.

Thomas W. Strong, printer
Signed: Howard Del

Abe Lincoln flattering himself on his chance of Re-election.

ABE LINCOLN FLATTERING HIMSELF ON HIS CHANCE OF RE-ELECTION

⇽ 1864 ⇾

The presidential race of 1864 was seen as a mandate on whether the war should continue. Casualties were mounting and the administration had called for a new draft of 500,000 men. This cartoon suggests that Lincoln was cocky about his chances of winning re-election, but Lincoln privately doubted that he would win. Jeff Davis did not have to worry about re-election since the Confederate Constitution called for a six-year term with no second term possible.

Southern Punch
Artist unknown

Long ABRAHAM LINCOLN a Little Longer.

LONG ABRAHAM LINCOLN A LITTLE LONGER

⊷⇒ 1864 ⇐⊶

Lincoln won re-election in 1864 with Andrew Johnson as his running mate. Lincoln carried all but three states—New Jersey, Kentucky, and Delaware—but the popular vote was close. Recent Union victories helped Lincoln in the election. With Lincoln a little longer, the North hoped the war would come to an end.

Harper's Weekly
(November 26)
Artist: Frank Bellew

BELLYCOSE APPEARANCE OF OUR BRAVE BOYS AFTER THANKSGIVING

⇥ 1864 ⇤

By Thanksgiving of 1864, it is hard to imagine that any soldier would have had much to be thankful for except that he had not been killed during the past summer and fall when some of the bloodiest fighting of the war took place.

Harper's Weekly
(December 3)
Artist: Frank Bellew

BELLYCOSE APPEARANCE OF OUR BRAVE BOYS AFTER THANKSGIVING.

A DOVE OF PEACE.

A DOVE OF PEACE

⇒ 1864 ⇐

In 1864, former General George McClellan ran on the Democratic Presidential ticket and though he did not officially endorse the "peace at any cost" platform, he was perceived as an advocate of negotiation with the Confederates. This cartoon calls attention to his abiguous position. He is portrayed as a dove of peace with an olive branch in his mouth, but he also holds a sword.

Frank Leslie's Illustrated Newspaper
(December 10)
Artist unknown

1865

SANTA CLAUS SHERMAN PUTTING SAVANNAH INTO UNCLE SAM'S STOCKING.

SANTA CLAUS SHERMAN PUTTING SAVANNAH INTO UNCLE SAM'S STOCKING

⇢═ 1865 ═⇠

After Sherman burned Atlanta in November 1864, he began his devastating "march to the sea" with a force of about 60,000. His troops captured Savannah on December 21, and Sherman offered the city to Lincoln as a Christmas present.

Frank Leslie's Illustrated Newspaper
(January 14)
Artist unknown

The Last Suggestion from Richmond

⚞ 1865 ⚟

A skeleton representing the Confederacy tries one last time to obtain recognition from France (Napoleon III) and England (John Bull), but to no avail.

Frank Leslie's Illustrated Newspaper
(January 28)
Artist: probably William Newman

THE LAST SUGGESTION FROM RICHMOND.

GHOST OF THE CONFEDERACY—"*I propose to throw myself under your protection—either joint-ly or separately.*"
BOTH—"*We don't see it. While you were a live person we might—but now you are a mere skeleton—nary—no—no,*"

JOHN BROWN EXHIBITING HIS HANGMAN:

JOHN BROWN EXHIBITING HIS HANGMAN

❖ 1865 ❖

In this cartoon, the abolitionist John Brown comes back from the dead to condemn Jeff Davis who sits in a bird cage attached to the gallows. Jeff Davis is portrayed in women's clothing and holds an apple. From the beginning of the war, Union soldiers sang about "hanging Jeff Davis from a sour apple tree." Below the cage, black men and women dressed like minstrels dance around and thumb their noses at him.

G. Querner, printer
Artist unknown

THE PEACE COMMISSION

⟜⇒ 1865 ⇐⟞

Throughout 1864, Jefferson Davis experienced opposition from his vice president, Alexander Stephens, and members of his cabinet over how he was conducting the war. This opposition culminated in calls for peace and an end to the war. Although much of the peace talk was simply posturing to divide Northern opinion of the war and strengthen the Peace Democrats chances in 1864, it was perceived by many within the South as treasonous.

Harper's Weekly
(February 18)
Artist unknown

THE PEACE COMMISSION.
Flying to ABRAHAM'S Bosom.

UNCLE ABE'S VALENTINE SENT BY COLUMBIA.

AN ENVELOPE FULL OF BROKEN CHAINS.

UNCLE ABE'S
VALENTINE SENT BY
COLUMBIA

⇢≡ 1865 ≡⇠

Broken shackles and a
note about the Thirteenth
Amendment to the
Constitution, which prohibits
slavery, are sent to Lincoln as
a Valentine from Columbia,
who represents the Union.

**Frank Leslie's Illustrated
News**
(February 25)
Artist: Thomas Nast

JEFF DAVIS "CALMLY CONTEMPLATING."

"Our country is now environed with perils which it is our duty calmly to contemplate."—
Extract from Davis's last Message.

JEFF DAVIS "CALMLY CONTEMPLATING"

⇒ 1865 ⇐

This cartoon mocks Jeff Davis for suggesting his country calmly con-template its situation since in fact it was on the precipice of losing the war. But calmness and gentility marked the surrender of Lee to Grant, after four years of devastation and bloodshed, and just nine days after this cartoon ran.

Harper's Weekly
(April 1)
Artist unknown

THE LAST DITCH OF THE CHIVALRY, OR A PRESIDENT IN PETTICOATS.

Published by Currier & Ives. 152 Nassau St. N.Y.

THE LAST DITCH OF THE CHIVALRY

⟨≡ 1865 ≡⟩

When Jeff Davis was captured by Federal cavalry near Irwinsville, Georgia on May 10, 1865 he was purportedly wearing women's clothes. The story goes that in an effort to escape capture, he had put on his wife's coat, supposedly by mistake. Then his wife put a shawl over his head. Cartoonists had a field day with the image of the fleeing former president of the Confederate States of America masquerading as a woman. Many put him in full female attire including a hoop skirt. In this cartoon, he tries to escape with Confederate gold.

Currier & Ives
Artist unknown

A Man Knows a Man

☞ 1865 ☜

A white Confederate soldier, at left, and an African American Union soldier shake hands as a sign of peace and understanding of each other's losses. The cartoon strives to show the sides as equal. Each man has lost a leg, each man is in uniform, and each man has crutch. The artist does not make clear who is speaking. This narrative ambiguity has the affect of making the North and South seem of one mind.

Harper's Weekly
(April 22)
Artist unknown

A MAN KNOWS A MAN.

"Give me your hand, Comrade! We have each lost a LEG for the good cause; but, thank GOD, we never lost HEART."

ABOUT THE SIZE OF IT.

UNCLE SAM. "Stand clear there, all airth and ocean! My hands are free now, and I'm goin' to hyst a flag so big that it'll cover most o' the land and a good bit o' the sea!"

In this optimistic and patriotic cartoon, the sun smiles down on the reunited United States, on Uncle Sam, and on the flag.

Harper's Weekly
(May 13)
Artist unknown

JEFFERSON DAVIS AS AN UNPROTECTED FEMALE!

"He is one of those rare types of humanity born to control destiny, or to accept, without murmur, annihilation as the natural consequence of failure."—*N. Y. Daily News, May 15, 1865.*

JEFFERSON DAVIS AS AN UNPROTECTED FEMALE!

⟶ 1865 ⟵

In this "Jeff in skirts" cartoon, Davis holds a water bucket labeled C.S. for the Confederate States. The water bucket figured into many of these cartoons because when Davis tried to elude his captors he took with him a black servant who carried a water bucket.

Harper's Weekly
(May 27)
Artist unknown

A PROPER FAMILY RE-UNION.

A PROPER FAMILY RE-UNION

⟶ 1865 ⟵

Benedict Arnold—a traitor from the American Revolution—and Satan stir a cauldron of "Treason Toddy" and welcome Jeff Davis into their company. Davis, dressed in women's clothing, stands near stolen gold and a suitcase bearing his initials and "C.S.A. 1865." A skull labeled "Andersonville" and one labeled "Libby" lie below the cauldron. Two copperhead snakes representing Peace Democrats are also on the ground.

Printer unknown
Artist: Burgoo Zac

JEFF'S LAST SHIFT.

Published by Currier & Ives. 152 Nassau St. N.Y.

JEFF'S LAST SHIFT

⇸ 1865 ⇷

In this cartoon, a civilian chides a Union soldier for mocking Jeff Davis. The soldier's response, "Who is he President of?" underscores that when Davis was captured, the Confederate States of America ceased to exist.

Currier & Ives
Artist: John Cameron

"AIN'T YOU GOING TO *RECOGNIZE* ME?"

"AIN'T YOU GOING TO *RECOGNIZE* ME?"

◆━ 1865 ━◆

Emporer Napolean III looks past Jeff Davis, and John Bull turns his back on him, signifying that the Confederate States of America would never be recognized as a nation.

Harper's Weekly
(June 3)
Signed: L. W. W.

Uncle Sam's Menagerie

⊸⊸ 1865 ⊸⊸

After Lincoln's assassination, the U.S. government suggested that the conspirators were agents of Jefferson Davis. Never charged with a crime, Davis was nonetheless imprisoned for two years in Virginia. In this cartoon, eight birds in nooses represent the accused. Among them is a skull labeled Booth: John Wilkes Booth, Lincoln's assassin, who shot himself rather than be captured. Uncle Sam stands before a cage holding Jeff Davis, who has the body of a hyena.

Publisher unknown
Artist unknown

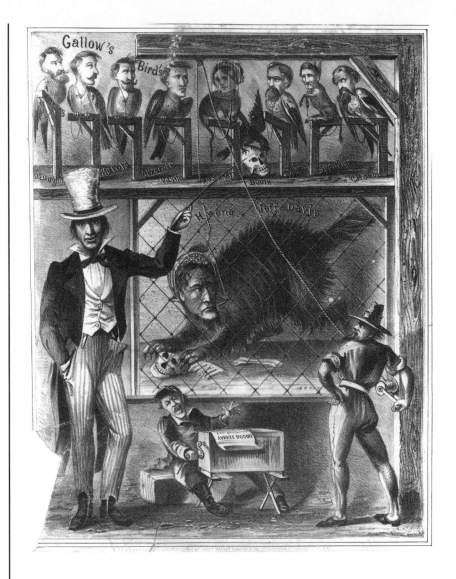

FINALE of the "JEFF DAVIS DIE-NASTY."
"Last Scene of all, that ends this strange eventful History."

FREEDOM'S IMMORTAL TRIUMPH!

⇢ 1865 ⇠

From the beginning of the war, Northern soldiers sang about hanging Jeff Davis from a sour apple tree.

Here, Davis receives that punishment. Satan peers out of an open grave while Justice sits in the clouds. Other Confederates are lined up to be hanged. Prisons can be seen in the background. At left, Liberty sits near an urn, partially covered by a Union flag with a grieving soldier and a sailor at the base. A former slave and his family reach out to Justice and toward Lincoln, who is being escorted to heaven by angels.

Charles Porah, printer
Artist: Burgoo Zac

TESTING THE QUESTION

—= 1865 =—

Many slaveholders were surprised that their newly freed slaves did not want to stay on the plantations where they were held in servitude. After the war, some former slave owners were taken aback when African Americans showed an interest in reuniting their families and claiming their liberty.

Harper's Weekly

(August 12)

Artist unknown

TESTING THE QUESTION.

Mrs. Randolphus (*a descendant of* Pocahontas, *and former owner of many slaves*). "Here, Uncle Tom, go down to the Tavern and tell your master I want him."

Uncle Tom. "No, I won't. I ain't your Uncle or your Arnty any more: I'se your Ekle" (equal)!

CHEAP—VERY.

A. J. OFFERS SOME DECIDED BARGAINS.

Even Confederate military and political leaders were allowed pardons with no restrictions in Andrew Johnson's Reconstruction plan. After the war, Southern states were able to put most of the conventions of the Old South easily back into place.

Frank Leslie's Illustrated Newspaper
(November 11)
Artist: probably William Newman

Illustration Credits

The editor and publisher are grateful to the following for permission to reproduce cartoons in their collections. Images may be protected by copyright. No images may be reproduced or distributed in any form without their permission.

The **University of Georgia Hargrett Rare Book and Manuscript Library** (Athens, Georgia) for images appearing on the following pages:
14, 22, 24, 25, 27, 28, 29, 30, 31, 32, 33, 37, 38, 39, 41, 42, 43, 44, 45, 46, 47, 48, 50, 51, 52, 56, 58, 59, 60, 64, 66, 67, 68, 69, 71, 74, 75, 76, 82, 83, 84, 85, 86, 87, 89, 90, 91, 92, 94, 95, 97, 102, 109, 110, 112, 114, 115, 116, 117, 118, 119, 120, 123, 125, 126, 127, 128, 131, 132, 133, 137, 138, 140, 141, 142, 144, 145, 146, 149, 152, 153

The **Maryland Historical Society** (Baltimore, Maryland) for images on the following pages:
19, 88, 99, 101,

The **Museum of the City of New York** (New York, New York) for images appearing on the following pages:
143, 148

The **Museum of the Confederacy** (Richmond, Virginia) for images appearing on the following pages:
20, 35, 96, 103, 108, 111, 130

The **New York Public Library**, General Research Division, Astor, Lenox, and Tilden Foundations (New York, New York) for images appearing on the following pages:
15, 21, 26,49, 55, 57, 62, 63, 65, 70, 72, 73, 77, 81, 93, 98

The **United States Library of Congress** (Washington, D.C.) for images appearing on the following pages:
3, 4, 5, 6, 7, 8, 9, 10, 13, 16, 17, 18, 22, 23, 34, 36, 40, 61, 100, 107, 113, 121, 122, 124, 129, 139, 147, 150, 151